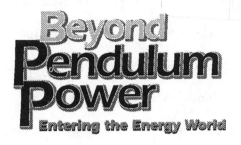

Beyond Pendulum Power
Entering the Energy World

"The best book on Pendulum Power on the market."
The Book Reader,
America's Most Independent Review of Books

Discover the energy world and tune in to reality.
Feel the frequencies and know using the pendulum.

If you are a New Ager this book is a must. It not only takes you
step by step to pendulum proficiency, but also specifically
guides you into the New Age...the next step in evolution:
becoming an energy being.

"**BEYOND PENDULUM POWER** is a totally new dimension
in dowsing. it presents for the first time many challenging
ideas for personal growth and development."
From the Preface by Virginia Baker
Trustee Emeritus, The American Society of Dowsers, Inc.
Founder and past president of the
Orange County California Chapter ASD

OTHER BOOKS BY GREG NIELSEN

Pyramid Power (co-author, Max Toth)

Pendulum Power (co-author, Joseph Polansky)

Tuning to the Spiritual Frequencies

MetaBusiness: Creating a New Global Culture

Beyond Pendulum Power
Entering the Energy World

"The best book on Pendulum Power
on the market."
—The Book Reader

By
Greg Nielsen

Conscious Books

Reno, Nevada

U S A

Conscious Books

316 California Ave., Suite 210
Reno, Nevada 89509

U S A

Copyright © 1988, Greg Nielsen

10 9 8 7 6 5 4 3 2

Library of Congress Catalog Card Number: 88-70068

ISBN 0-9619917-0-4

Printed and Bound in The United States of America

Cover art by Terralin Carroll

Cover designed at WHITE SAGE STUDIOS
Virginia City, Nevada

To Dane

and

The American Society of Dowsers, Inc.
Danville, Vermont 05828-0024

Acknowledgments

I am grateful for the interest and support generously given by Joanie Ward, Dee Totten, and Tom Anderson. Thank you Vitvan and The School of the Natural Order, Baker, Nevada 89311 for permission to quote and reprint figure 1. Write and request the Vitvan book list. Thanks also to Fritjof Capra for permission to quote from The Tao of Physics. Jennie I appreciate your typing. Mom, thanks for your editing job. Dad, thanks for always believing in me. Carol Ackerman, your line drawings were a big help. Terri Carroll, your cover art is an inspiration! Randy, I appreciate your cover layout. Keith Johnson, your patience and assistance was a godsend. Bob Bosler, your design, layout and typesetting brought everything together, thanks a million. Virginia, the Preface gave me encouragement. Izzy, Organics was a lifesaver; I am deeply grateful.

TABLE OF CONTENTS

Text

Illustrations

PREFACE

Humanity now stands on the threshold of a new age: *The Age of Aquarius. The Age of Aquarius is about to usher in new concepts about life and reality. Each of us must now make decisions; either to accept and enjoy the new journey and the new challenges it presents to us, or to desperately hang on to the old ideas and continue the struggle of past ages.*

Dowsing, the art of searching for unseen objects with the aid of a hand held object, has been used throughout the ages to successfully locate water, minerals or anything else of the material realm that was missing or needed. In the Piscean Age, material needs were all important, but now mankind is discovering more and more that the finer energies, those of the unseen world, are of great importance to our health, happiness and success in life.

Beyond Pendulum Power is a totally new dimension in dowsing. It presents for the first time many challenging ideas for personal growth and development. No longer will the dowser's search be for "things" on the outside, but using his dowsing ability, tune into the energies that create and sustain life - call it spirit, life force, Christ power, light or whatever you will.

Seerers and sages of all ages have tuned into this same God Power and given the world the wisdom needed at that time for the development and advancement of the race. Now, all persons who will take the time to develop their own consciousness can have the ability to "tune-in" to the "great computer in the sky," to worlds beyond our five senses.

Pendulum Dowsing is a method for turning within for the answers to our every need. You will discover within you the TRUTH, and as Jesus said, "The TRUTH shall set you free." Knowing the TRUTH is the first step to overcoming all errors. After TRUTH comes understanding, love and forgiveness.

The future is in your hands, literally! Develop your dowsing knowledge and skill then watch the light grow in your life. "You are the LIGHT of the world." Now, read and enjoy this most informative book, develop your dowsing power and let the light be your guide.

Virginia Baker
Trustee emeritus, The American Society of Dowsers, Inc.
Founder and past President of the Orange County California
Chapter ASD

CHAPTER 1: BEYOND PENDULUM POWER

It was the spring of 1972. I was almost 24. In an apartment on West 78th Street on Manhattan's upper west side a friendly man introduced me to the pendulum.

Before I give you my reaction to this first experience with the pendulum, let me give you a little background leading up to this meeting.

In January of 1970, I was vacationing in Laguna Beach, California. I traveled to Southern California from Minnesota with the thought of possibly moving there permanently.

The sixties were over, I was still on a spiritual quest. The Southern California area was a hotbed for any number of cults, groups, centers and communes.

While I enjoyed the beach, the sun and the salt air I crossed paths with the Friends-of-the-Desert, the Hare Krishnas, vegetarians, a yoga group and the born again Christians.

I lived next door to a carpenter and his wife who practiced yoga and vegetarianism. He just got out of prison for dealing marijuana. They introduced me to a book titled, **The Path of the Masters.**

At the end of three weeks my consciousness had definitely changed. I called a woman friend of mine in New York City and talked about my experiences. She and her sister had found a guru - a spiritual teacher.

She told me to hold on. She put him on the phone. His name was Francois. Our conversation was quite interesting; so interesting that I asked if I could come to New York and study with him. He said alright.

A week later I was living in an old hotel in Greenwich Village. My training under Francois began. From February 1970 until his death in October 1971 I studied non-stop, learning some of the basics of the ancient gnostic sciences.

Before Francois' early death, I had met the friendly man at Francois' apartment on West 78th Street. He gave us a talk on structure, function and order. His talk was fascinating.

After Francois' death I kept in contact with the friendly man from Brooklyn. He seemed to have some specific and practical steps to follow on the spiritual path.

Still, it was not until that warm spring day in 1972 that he introduced me to the pendulum.

"Greg, have you ever heard of the pendulum?" he queried in a gruff Brooklyn accent as he reached into his pants pocket.

"No....no," I answered with a defensive tone. I had much more intellectual pride then than now. I know he didn't mean the kind of pendulum that keeps accurate time.

From his small stubby hand dropped an oblong wooden thing. It dangled from the black string he held firmly.

"Here, go ahead and hold it." He saw the curiosity in my eyes.

He handed it to me. I held the string, rotating the oblong piece of wood.

"Do you want to try an experiment," my teacher asked forcefully?

"Sure," I said not sure I was sure.

"Here, sit at this desk. Draw a large plus sign on this piece of paper."

"Now hold the pendulum steady over the plus sign with the pendulum suspended directly over the point where the vertical and horizontal cross. Concentrate on the pendulum directing it with your mind along the vertical line."

It moved along the vertical! I smiled and laughed. I stopped it. I made it move along the horizontal. The pendulum world opened, a vast universe of potential knowledge to be explored. (See Chapter 4: How to Use the Pendulum for complete instructions on mind over matter experiment.)

Then my teacher showed me the yes/no questioning techniques. I was on my way. I seemed to take to the pendulum like fish to water and birds to air. Many of the answers I received were accurate giving me the confidence to go on.

But also many answers I found to be inaccurate prompting me to investigate and practice more.

From the spring of 1972 to the fall of 1975 was an intense learning cycle with the pendulum. I read everything I could get my hands on.

I was surprised and excited by the research and instruction given by the French priests like Abbe Mermet. The British were also active in researching and writing about the pendulum. There was a wealth of information and a lot to practice those three and a half years.

In the fall of 1975 Warner/Destiny Books contacted me and my fellow pendulumist, Joseph Polansky, requesting we write a mass market paperback on the pendulum. We were ready, willing and able. We began work on **Pendulum Power** immediately.

We completed the book in the summer of 1976 and it was published in February of 1977. **Pendulum Power** was reviewed in the May 1978 issue of the American Society of Dowsers Quarterly Digest, The American Dowser.

"The authors start off with a brief history of dowsing, some theories about the pendulum action and instructions in the use of the pendulum. Much of the

book is given over to detailed accounts of the uses of the pendulum in a way that will encourage the novice to practice and become proficient. Emphasis is placed on self-development through **Pendulum Power.**"

Cue Magazine, now New York Magazine, reviewed **Pendulum Power** in the May 14 - 27, 1977 issue.

"For a little more than plain old fun, get yourself a pendulum - and a book to go with it, **Pendulum Power** by Greg Nielsen and Joseph Polansky. According to the authors (who cite historical evidence):

"..the pendulum, when operated properly, can be used to read energy patterns, and consequently can be used to obtain answers to such personal questions as: will he marry me? Should I go to Spain next summer? Should I quit my job and join the roller derby? The book carefully goes through the steps of divining via the pendulum, which, incidently, can be easily made at home from an everyday object (e.g. a button and a piece of string). When you read how the pendulum was used to <u>detect enemy mines and tunnels in Vietnam</u> and used to find lost persons, you may lay your cynicism aside for a moment to test one of the oldest phenomenon known to man."

The November 1976 issue of Gentleman's Quarterly magazine, of all places, featured the pendulum's powers.

"The pendulum has been used for thousands of years as a tool to help man get in touch with his subconscious. Joseph Polansky, who, with Greg Nielsen, authored the book **Pendulum Power**, explains its effects this way. "The human nervous system is the most accurate sensor in the world. The nervous system responds to hundreds and thousands of frequencies of which the conscious mind is not aware. You can tune yourself into your nervous system by making a pendulum - any object that doesn't conduct electricity hung from a string - and programming yourself to receive information from it. Tell yourself that if the answer is "yes", the pendulum will swing clockwise, and if the answer if "no", the pendulum will swing counter-clockwise. You can diagnose yourself or a friend by making a list of organs and, concentrating on one organ at a time, asking if that organ is healthy. "Of course," Polansky cautions, "it can take as much as a year to become proficient. You have to make sure you're emotionally neutral about the situations; otherwise, you'll subconsciously influence the swing."

Naturally, it felt good when the public took an interest in the book. It motivated me to continue my efforts as a pendulumist.

From 1978 - 1981 I lived in Seagate, Brooklyn on the tip of Coney Island. I gave pendulum readings to my students. It was during these years that I graduated from the yes/no reading to the scale reading. It became evident to me that yes/no answers in the area of human life and living was too simplistic.

When my students proposed questions for me to answer with the pendulum I worded them as follows: on a 0 - 10 scale is it wise for (name) to (fill in the blank). This changed my position in relations to the student or anyone else asking for a reading. The answer was no longer in black or white terms - cut and dry. Instead, the person receiving the reading had to make the final decision. They had to use their own free will.

It was important to me as a teacher not to tell the student "THE" answer, it was more important to present the options and let the student make the choices.

So from 1978 on I have, especially in the areas of self-help, almost exclusively used the scale reading. This does not mean that in the beginning stages a novice pendulumist should avoid yes/no questions. Rather, it's advisable to begin with the yes/no questions and then graduate to the scale readings as one naturally feels ready.

During this four year stretch I used the pendulum almost on a daily basis as a tuning device. I tuned-in to my students before classes so I could do a better job. Obviously, if you have a beat on a student's mental-emotional-physical state chances are you can present information accordingly. Often I would scrap my planned lesson in favor of something totally different based on the vibration I picked up on when tuning with the pendulum.

Beside tuning for teaching, I was asked questions on job, career, business, health, relationships, lifestyle, travel, family, education ... the list goes on and on.

New worlds opened to me, my students and others who requested readings. It was even more evident to me that we lived in a dynamic energy world. When I asked a question and tuned-in to an answer I often felt a vibration a frequency, an energy which indicated to me an answer while the pendulum simultaneously moved in agreement with the feeling I picked up on.

This new experience meant that **I was the Pendulum!**

Whoever used the pendulum - novice, intermediate, advanced or master - was the pendulum. The weight hanging from a string was simply an extension of oneself as the experience.

From this realization it was a small jump in perception to the wider view that all humans are pendulums - **You are the pendulum!** You have the potential to consciously tune-in to anything, any place, any person and receive a vibration-feeling indicating the quality/level.

I am grateful for the opportunity to express my experiences with the pendulum. The greatest reward to me as pendulumist is if someone reads this book and learns how to tune-in to the energy world, gain self-knowledge, understanding and begins to plant the seeds of wisdom.

May the Spiritual Consciousness awaken in you.

Greg Nielsen

March, 1988

CHAPTER 2: YOU ARE THE PENDULUM!

Simple Harmonic Motion

Any vibratory motion which follows a regular and repeated pattern is called a simple harmonic motion. A tuning fork, a bouncing ball, the turning of wheels and a swinging pendulum are examples of simple harmonic motion.

The story goes that young Galileo was attending church one Sunday in Pisa, Italy in 1581. Being an acute observer, he set his eyes on the church's chandelier. It seemed to move back and forth at precisely the same intervals.

Galileo used the simple harmonic motion of his heart beat, checking his pulse, to verify his observation. The idea for the pendulum clock was conceived. Accurate time keeping was now possible.

Still, the first successful pendulum clock was not invented until the 17th century by the great Dutch astronomer, Christian Huygens. The constant and regular oscillation of the pendulum allowed scientists to measure more accurately.

So what does simple harmonic motion and the invention of the pendulum clock have to do with you and I?

As human beings with the potential for becoming conscious - awareness of thoughts, feelings, desires and emotions and how they are linked to the activities and events in our life - we are human harmonic motions and living pendulums.

As humans each of us has a unique harmonic motion, a kind of life rhythm, which, if we follow it, brings us the treasures of love, satisfying work and spiritual insight. If we do not find and follow our individual natural rhythm then suffering becomes our unwanted companion.

When we are out of sync, off rhythm, the unwanted companions - suffering, frustration, pain and disease - shadow us until we get back on track, until we find our individual rhythm and follow it.

Living rhythmically, in simple harmonic motion, means you are more spiritually tuned. Your intuition is more precise, more right on. In addition, your awareness is clearer; you see what's happening.

In this state of being you are a measurer, a seer of what is. In fact you are a pendulum! The pendulum, in the hand of a trained and experienced pendulumist is nothing more or less than a measurer of what is.

A conscious human, living in sync with their natural rhythm, is the measurer. The more conscious and rhythmic he or she is the more accurate the measurement. An accurate measurer knows. Knowledge is power. The measured application of that power is wisdom.

There's an ancient Hindu saying that goes something like this: "Where the measurer, the measured and the measurement meet there I am." In simple terms when you consciously measure life you are more centered. And when you are centered you feel the high frequency force of your being.

The Force of Balance

A weight at the end of a string, set it in motion and let gravity do the rest. The back and forth swing of a pendulum repeats at regular intervals.

Our psycho-spiritual natures do not usually vibrate so rhythmically. Gravity is not the only force. A host of psychological and spiritual forces are active within us.

In order to set the house in order each of us must make a decision to do so. Leaving it to chance, hoping we will "get it together" somehow or waiting for the most opportune time just are not effective strategies to becoming a living pendulum.

Balance is the force which most directs life toward rhythmic, pendulum-like living. A sense of balance, in the psycho-spiritual sense, means knowing when you have gone too far in one direction or, better still, when you're about to go too far in one direction. Then, at that point, turning your attention and, therefore, the flow of your life energies in another more balanced direction.

The story of a corporate president comes to mind here. As the head of a new venture company marketing a genius invention a tremendous responsibility rested on his shoulders.

Raising funds, paying bills, designing a marketing strategy, coordinating staff...his work load was endless.

He desperately wanted to see this baby business walk. Long hours in the office kept him away from home, wife, family and friends.

His work took on a kind of cursed obsession. Nothing was more important than the holy man at the office. He began to take full responsibility for the company's success or failure. Nothing else mattered but work.

My friend lost his psycho-spiritual balance. His attentions and energies flowed out of balance. The swing of his inner pendulum had become erratic; he was stuck on one end of the swing.

Now, without conscious alternation in natural rhythm to other activities, problems and frustrations increased in a geometric ratio.

My friend became physically run down, drained and lethargic. He felt pains in his stomach; his body was tensed; he had pains in his chest area.

These experiences woke him up! "What's happening?" he asked himself. He became aware of what he was doing to himself. He had lost his inner balance.

He took immediate steps. He spent more time away from the office. He practiced some meditation and relaxation exercises. He took some short trips for a change of scenery and finally, he changed his attitude toward work; he stopped placing the total burden of success or failure on his shoulders.

The force of gravity moves the physical pendulum back and forth. The force of balance moves our psycho-spiritual pendulum back and forth. And, as you learn how to tune-in using a pendulum, you'll discover the force of "What Is" sets the pendulum into motion.

The Psycho-Spiritual Nature

As an apprentice pendulumist you must get in touch with your psycho-spiritual nature.

Before I go on - what do I mean by "psycho-spiritual nature."? There are vibrations we all experience psychologically and there are vibrations we experience spiritually.

Some of the psychological vibrations include:

Thinking	Feeling	Desire
Thought	Mood	Want
Ideas	Emotion	Need
Mental Activity	Like	Fear
Imagination	Dislike	Guilt
Fantasy	Fight	Etc.

Some of the spiritual vibrations include:

Consciousness	Wisdom	Clarity
Understanding	Creativity	Light
Forgiveness	Gratitude	Strength
Faith	Giving	Health
Peace	Will	Transmutation
Love	Compassion	Etc.

The psychological and spiritual natures are interrelated, they are artificially separated by our minds. In reality they are inseparable. That's why I connect the two words with a hypen.

A psyche without spiritual vibrations is like a city without traffic lights. The spiritual frequencies bring equilibrium and stability to the psyche. An apprentice pendulumist cannot become a journeyman or master pendulumist without tuning and experiencing the spiritual frequencies

The psycho-spiritual vibrations are felt and experienced but not seen by the physical eye. The effects of these vibrations can be seen on the physiological structure - the body.

Someone going through trauma, turmoil and terror is experiencing chaos in the psyche. The effects on the body can be seen in the form of muscle tension, drooping shoulders, darkness in the eyes, frowning and so on.

A pendulumist must, I repeat, **must** become conscious of the psycho-spiritual vibrations they experience. Begin today practicing self-observation. Stop for just a few seconds, close your eyes and observe the thoughts that pop into your mental field. Do this for about 10 or 15 seconds non-stop. Go ahead.

What did you notice? Did any thoughts pop into your mental field. Did you catch them? Did you remember what they were? You have started the process of self-observation.

A pendulumist must be keenly conscious of the psycho-spiritual vibrations moving within. Their unconscious activity while doing pendulum readings can alter the reading enough to make it inaccurate.

The first step in calming the inner forces is awareness of their activity. Everyday must be devoted to gradually becoming more and more conscious of the "inner forces".

Refer to the list of psychological/spiritual vibrations on page 9. Are you conscious of the vibrations at the moment at which you experience them?

Begin self-observation practices today. Stop for 30 seconds at least once an hour and observe your thoughts, your feelings, your moods, your emotions and your bodily tensions.

Observe yourself when you're creative, loving, grateful, giving and understanding. Consciously experience the experience.

A Living Pendulum

Take a weighted object, attach it to a flexible length of string, chain or cord and suspend it from a fixed point and you have a pendulum.

We are all living pendulums. By correspondence the weight is your body, the flexible length is the silver cord connecting you to the flexible fixed point of your being.

The "silver cord" is your lifeline to the nourishing and sustaining frequencies of spiritual vibration, "manna from heaven". Have you ever watched an astronaut on television take a space walk? Did you notice the long cord attached from the spacecraft to his space suit? That is his lifeline, his silver cord to the life sustaining space shuttle.

While in a physical body we are subject to the laws of the physical plane; gravity holds us to the earth. We feel the pull of gravity as weight.

We, however, are more than a body. We have a soul. The life of the soul depends on the spiritual vibrations that flow down the silver cord.

The soul life needs harmony, love, peace, balance and creativity to grow and to accomplish its appointed tasks.

When we identify with the body to the exclusion of the soul and spirit we build up a negative resistance in the soul. As a result, the currents descending from spiritual dimensions by way of the transmission line, the silver cord, meet the resistance in the soul.

Having reduced the flow of higher force, we become slaves to sense. We are overly fascinated by the glitter and glamour. We live for pleasure. Fulfilling bodily desires is our motivation, compulsion and obsession.

A weighted object without a flexible length of string connected to a stable point is useless as a pendulum. It cannot oscillate back and forth rhythmically. It cannot keep time; it measures nothing.

Humans who have disconnected themselves from the rich experiences of a soul life with the accompanying force, strength and vitality of spiritual vibration feel useless inside. Their lives do not pulsate with rhythmic alternation and oscillation. They are unconscious. They cannot measure their ways. The light of consciousness dims. They are blind.

If we discover and realize the body is just one vehicle through which consciousness operates, its needs, desires and sensations become less important. Our attention turns then to what's more important, the spiritual life.

Our center, our being, our cosmic heritage can be found only in the stable connection to the source of life, The Presence, the limitless clear light of consciousness.

A human who does not become centered in the spiritual life is not a living pendulum. Your accuracy with the pendulum is directly related to your level of consciousness, level of skill and level of being.

Your first priority as a pendulumist is being tuned up and tuned-in. Next, become conscious of the correspondence between your structure as a body-soul-spirit (living pendulum) and the weight-flexible length-fixed point of the pendulum dowsing tool and finally, be aware that it's a **process** of self-evolution and illumination as well as a **process** of learning how to use the pendulum as a tuning device.

The Pendulum Antenna

Tools are an extension of the body, brain and nervous system. A hoe and shovel are extensions of the hands, and far more efficient than hands. The computer is an extension of the brain, saving us time and energy that can be used more productively.

The pendulum is simply an extension of the nervous system, especially the sympathetic nervous system. The sympathic nervous system specializes in registering feelings. When you walk into a room and feel excitement in the air the sympathic nervous system is working. You cannot see or touch the excitement but you definitely experience it.

The pendulum functions as an antenna to the sensitive sympathetic system. By holding the pendulum attentively and asking a specific, meaningful question you are increasing the clarity of reception. The conscious tuning-in to vibrations heightens sensitivity to subtle experiences.

At this very moment, as I write, television sounds/images are passing through the room. The TV set is not on. I cannot see them but they are being broadcast.

Once the set is turned on the antenna picks up the image and you see the pictures. Once you turn on your attention, ask your question and hold out the pendulum you can pick up the vibrational answer to the question.

Have you ever turned on your television with the rabbit ears down? Fuzz - the picture is unclear. Put the rabbit ears up, clarity.

The pendulum functions precisely like a television antenna. Hold the pendulum out and tune the channel of your attention to a specific frequency and you become a human television.

Now, as you practice using the pendulum, refining the receptivity of your sympathetic nervous system, you become more like a TV set hooked up to a roof antenna. The reception becomes crystal clear. Answers to questions are obvious. You will definitely experience the vibrational feel of the answer with accompanying images and words.

The television/antenna analogy is excellent for another most important reason. You can turn off the television with the push of a button. You can put down the pendulum and stop tuning-in to particular vibrations.

There can be nothing more agonizing, horrifying or draining than turning on psychic awareness and leaving it on without the switch to turn it off. The sympathetic nervous system would be over-taxed. Exceeding its NTP, Normal Temperature and Pressure, it would breakdown. Emotional obsessions, mental aberration and physical disease may result.

Using the pendulum teaches you to turn tunings on and off. The control factor takes you beyond "psychic sensationalism" into spiritual purpose.

Today psychic sensationalism is rampant. The race psyches of the earth are polluted with psychic garbage just as the oceans of the earth are polluted with all manner of poisons.

When you tune-in consciously, as you learn to do with the pendulum, you are more in control of the psychic forces. What you're conscious of you tend to control.

With unconscious tuning, as in sensational psychism, the psychic forces tend to control you. There is a choice.

Unconscious Tuning: A Woman is Temporarily Crippled

I received a phone call from an anxious woman one morning. She was calling from her hospital bed.

"Greg, I'm in the hospital," she blurted out.

"What happened?" I questioned wanting to find out the facts.

"Yesterday I was listening to a meditation, relaxation tape. I was in deep relaxation when the phone rang startling me back to reality. I got up to answer the phone and my legs gave out. I had to crawl to get to the phone. It was my husband." She paused to get her breath.

"Go on, I'm listening," I said.

"I told him my legs were kind of numb, I couldn't walk and I had to crawl to answer the phone. He rushed home, carried me to the car and drove me to the hospital.

The doctors could not find anything wrong. My legs were still numb; I could not walk. I checked into the hospital for tests. That was yesterday. They cannot find a thing."

I questioned this confused, panic stricken woman further. A psychiatrist had been assigned to her case. There was nothing physically wrong (although she couldn't walk) so it had to be psychosomatic.

Here is just one example - **unconscious tuning is dangerous**. The woman passively opened herself up to suggestions coming from the person recorded on tape. She abdicated her free will.

Just before the phone rang the person on tape said, "now relax your legs - first the left leg,now the right. Feel them go numb.

Ring ... ing ... ing ... ing.

The phone ringing drove the suggestion, "feel them go numb," deep into the subconscious. The subconscious is like an adolescent who doesn't know any better. It accepts suggestions without discrimination. The suggestion acted like a command phrase and her body responded accordingly. She could not walk.

Anyway, I advised the woman to first throw out all tranquilizers no matter what the doctors and nurses said. When she called me she was drugged, mumbling and stumbling her words. I could feel the groggy vibration over the phone.

Next, I told her to write the phrase, "now feel your legs go numb," on a piece of paper. Then for 20 minutes touch it with both hands for a second and let go for a second.

She did that two days in a row. By the third day she was able to walk some. The right leg was worse than the left, but she was able to manage. She checked out of the hospital. She repeated the touch-and-let-go exercise several more times. It took several weeks before her legs completely recovered.

I had her send me the relaxation tape. I listened to part of it; that's all I could take. The person on the tape emitted an unconscious, hypnotic vibration which made you feel like you were being "put under" against your will. The tape is now available somewhere in the New York City dump.

The woman did not have control of what entered or exited her consciousness. She, with all good intentions, abdicated her awareness throne. Afterall, she reasoned, "all I wanted to learn was how to relax." Still, the fact remains, she unconsciously allowed someone elses consciousness to "relax" her not her own consciousness.

With the pendulum you consciously choose to tune-in. You turn your consciousness, tuning-in. You consciously register the quality of force, frequency and field. And finally, you consciously turn off your tuning-in and put the pendulum down.

Passive psychism is dangerous. Conscious tuning is a light in the darkness.

SUMMARY

1. Any vibratory motion that follows a regular and repeated pattern is a simple harmonic motion.

2. As humans, each of us has an individual harmonic motion, a kind of life rhythm, which, if we follow it, brings us the treasures of love, satisfying work and spiritual insight.

3. If we do not find and follow our individual natural rhythm, then suffering becomes our unwanted companion.

4. The pendulum, in the hand of a trained, experienced and conscious pendulumist, is nothing more or less than a measurer of what is.

5. When you consciously measure life you are more centered. And when you are centered you feel the high frequency force of your being.

6. Balance is the force which must direct life toward rhythmic, pendulum-like living.

7. A sense of balance, in the psycho-spiritual sense, means knowing when you have gone too far in one direction or, better still, when you're about to go too far in one direction.

8. The force of gravity moves the physical pendulum back and forth. The force of balance moves our psycho-spiritual pendulum back and forth.

9. An apprentice pendulumist must get in touch with their psycho-spiritual nature.

10. A psyche without spiritual vibrations is like a city without traffic lights.

11. A pendulumist must be keenly conscious of the psycho-spiritual vibrations moving within. Their unconscious activity while doing a pendulum reading can alter the reading enough to make it inaccurate.

12. We are all living pendulums. By correspondence the weight is our body, the flexible length is the silver cord and the fixed point is our being.

13. Our center, our being, our cosmic heritage can be found only in the continuous connection to the source of life, The Presence, the limitless clear light of consciousness.

14. Your accuracy with the pendulum is directly related to your level of consciousness, level of skill and level of being.

15. The pendulum functions precisely like a television antenna. Hold the pendulum out and tune the channel of your attention to a specific frequency and you become a human television.

16. Using the pendulum teaches you to turn tunings on and off. The control factor takes you beyond "psychic sensationalism" into spiritual purpose.

17. With unconscious tuning as in sensational psychism, the psychic forces tend to control you. There **is** a choice. Conscious tuning is a light in the darkness.

CHAPTER 3: FREQUENCIES, FORCES, FIELDS

Welcome to the Energy World

How frequently does your heart beat? How frequently do you inhale-exhale? How frequently does the sun rise and set?

Sound, light, thought and love - every person, place and thing, the invisible and the visible - All That Is vibrates at a specific cycle per unit of time.

Take your pulse. If your heart beats from 60 - 80 beats per minute while at rest, that's a fairly regular "frequency". After dancing, jogging or swimming your heart rate may increase temporarily to 120 beats per second; the "frequency" may double.

Look at the chart of the known electro-magnetic spectrum on page 18, figure 1. You will see some familiar words like radio, FM television, heat and X-rays. All of these **invisible** wavelengths and energies shape our daily lives.

Imagine for just a moment daily life without the harnessing of radio, television and microwaves. You would instantly ride a timemachine back to the early 20th century. Take away the harnessing of x-rays and many dental and medical procedures would be barbaric by today's standards. Contemplate World War II without radar!

Now look near the middle of the chart. Do you see the word "visible"? Of the known and still unknown (to science) frequencies, the narrow slit of visible frequencies that you and I see is like looking through a keyhole at the cosmos.

Fritjof Capra wrote in the **Tao of Physics,**

"Light is nothing but a rapidly alternating electromagnetic field traveling through space in the form of waves. Today we know that radio waves, light waves, and x-rays are all electromagnetic waves, oscillating electric and magnetic fields differing only in the frequency of their oscillation, and that visible light is only a tiny fraction of the electromagnetic spectrum."

Welcome to the energy world where you venture beyond the world of the five senses, beyond what you can see, hear, taste, smell and touch.

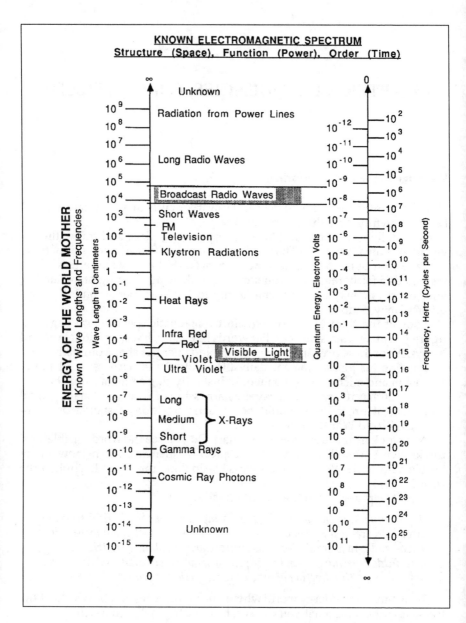

Figure 1: Known Electro-Magnetic Spectrum.

Using the pendulum, you can explore the infinite, multidimensional vastness of the energy world. You can tune-in to the visible thousands of miles away or the visible right where you are. When you become conscious in the energy world all-knowing becomes available to you. You simply tune-in to the frequency or frequencies and you register, experience and know.

Vitvan, a 20th century American Master, pioneered and explored vast regions of the frequency world. In his **Basic Teachings of the School of the Natural Order: Volume 1** he wrote:

> *"We live in an "ocean" of energy frequencies. Our awareness of these frequencies depends upon our ability to register them. This ability we can develop as certainly as we can tune-in on vibrations or radio frequencies with a radio. Receptivity counts heavily here: what we get depends, in one instance, on the radio, and in the other, on one's state of awareness."*

Vitvan found the key that unlocks the door to limitless worlds - direct perception, direct experience, direct knowing. Becoming a pendulumist **is one method of many** of exploring the energy world.

The American Master also wrote:

> *"Every sensation, every feeling, every emotion, every urge and every thought that you experience or that you think you have, is due to the registry of energy - wavelengths and frequencies. ...Our great work is to develop the consciousness of frequencies registered... there is an infinite range of wavelengths and frequencies to explore, to register and to know. Each can say for himself, "that of which I am now conscious is due to my ability to register wavelengths and frequencies." No one can give you this. You must develop it for yourself. As I cannot eat food to nourish your body, so I cannot endow you with a high-level knowing."*

You and **no one else** can cultivate the physical repose, emotional calm, peace of mind and focused tuning necessary to become a pendulumist. As a conscious pendulumist you can travel to inner and outer space. You can tune-in to the planets and the stars or the thoughts and intentions of earth leaders. Nothing is hidden. All things shall be revealed to experiencers of the energy world.

Again, welcome to the energy world.

Forces

In the energy world there are four forces. A force is energy in motion following a repetitious pattern. Physicists and alchemists describe and name the 4 forces differently. Yet there are also similarities. By the law of harmonic correspondence you will see physics and alchemy are not in conflict.

Forces: The Physicist

The physicist categorizes the four forces of the universe as follows, from strongest to weakest.

1. Nuclear Force
2. Electro-magnetic Force
3. Weak Force (decay reactions)
4. Gravitational Force

The nuclear forces, by far the most powerful in nature, hold positively charged protons and neutral neutrons together. This strong interaction occurs in the nucleus of every atom with the power of ten million electron volts.

Second in strength, yet substantially less powerful, (100 times weaker than the nuclear force) is the electromagnetic force. Electromagnetism is the interaction between charged particles. In the atom the attraction between positive protons and negative electrons holds the atom together. Electromagnetic interactions are responsible for chemical processes and the resulting combinations of molecular structures.

One hundred million times weaker than the electromagnetic force is the weak force. The weak interactions occur in the subatomic world and are so weak they do not hold anything together. Rather, this force manifests in particle collisions and in particle decay reactions.

The weakest force in physics is the gravitional force. It interacts between all particles until on the macroscopic level gravitational interactions occur between massive heavenly bodies. It is the force that holds the earth in orbit around the sun.

Forces: The Alchemist

The alchemist also saw the cosmos as the interaction of 4 forces. They measured their strength from most to least volatile.

1. Fire
2. Air
3. Water
4. Earth

On an everyday physical/sensation level we all experience the four elements. In fact, we require all four to survive. Without fire we would freeze to death. Without air we would suffocate; without water we would dehydrate; and without earth we would have no tools or food.

The alchemist, who applied this knowledge to his own life, was more than a scientist. He was a gnostic initiate. A Gnostic is one who knows the way, goes the way and experiences the transmutation of base sense, emotion, desire and thought into the light of wisdom and love.

The gnostic-alchemist observed the activity and effects of the four elements and learned about the structure and order of the cosmos. They observed the four elements while considering the occult law: **as above so below.** The "as above" refers to invisible energy worlds. The "so below" refers to the sensory world.

The alchemist realized that the 4 elements on this level were a reflection of the 4 elements working on every level, every frequency band.

The four forces of physics, for example, correspond to the four forces of alchemy.

Physics	Alchemy
Nuclear Force	Fire
Weak Force	Air
Electromagnetic	Water
Gravitational	Earth

Contemplate the four natural elements; then re-read what was said about the four forces of physics. Do you see how they correspond?

The alchemist saw the workings of the four elements on the psychological level with the following correspondence.

Elements	Psyche
Fire	Spirit
Air	Thought
Water	Feeling
Earth	Sensation

Synthesis

Albert Einstein struggled half his life trying to develop a Unified Field Theory that integrated the nuclear force, weak force, electromagnetism and gravity. He was unsuccessful.

In the 1980's physicists from around the world flocked to Cern, the world capital of high-energy physics. Located at the foot of the Jura Mountains in Switzerland, Cern has the largest and most powerful atomic particle accelerator in the world, the superproton synchotron; 4.2 miles in circumference.

A 17 mile accelerator is under construction, the large electron positron collider.

What is the purpose of colliding subatomic particles approaching the speed of light? Physicists are trying to discover the unity of the four forces experimentally. Italian physicist, Carlo Rublia's discoveries link the weak and the electromagnetic forces.

While the 20th Century physicists struggle to unify the four forces, the alchemists achieved a synthesis hundreds and even thousands of years ago.

The alchemists' experiment was a mixing of the four elements in right measure and proportion. The resultant force they called the ether.

To them this mixing process was going on within the crucible of their individual psyches. Spirit, thought, feeling and sensation blending and balancing into a single force, a 5th element, ether; a stable psychological nature.

The alchemist, the gnostic, the initiate who harnesses the 4 elements of his psychic nature becomes a reflection of "Higher Force". A kind of etheric presence is felt as a peace, perception and strength all at once.

I have no doubt physicists will "rediscover" (as opposed to discover) a unified synthesis of the 4 forces. They will rediscover a fifth force, an ether which interpenetrates and intermingles the other four forces; they will call it "The Presence" because it is present universally.

What does knowing about forces have to do with learning to use the pendulum? Your knowledge and harnessing of the inner psychological forces of spirit-fire, thought-air, water-feeling and earth-sensation is,perhaps, 75% of mastering the pendulum.

Once you more or less harness your inner forces you will be able to more easily tune-in to the forces of others. Your steady self-control will give you access to the submicroscopic forces of physics. In short, the cosmos is your playground! Venture where you will consciously.

Fields

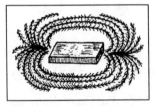

Figure 2: Pattern of iron filings near a magnet.

Almost everyone has seen what happens when you place iron filings on a sheet of paper and hold a magnet underneath the paper near the filings (see Figure 2 on the this page). You suddenly see the pattern of the magnetic lines of force. The invisible magnetic field is revealed.

We are surrounded, interpenetrated, integrated and sustained by the universal field. Magnetic fields, gravitational fields, electromagnetic fields, bio-fields, auric-fields - there are fields within fields within fields, all interlinked structurally and functionally.

The German particle physicist, W. Thirring, expressed it as follows:

"The field exists always and everywhere; it can never be removed. It is the carrier of all material phenomena. It is the "void" out of which the proton creates the pi-mesons. Being and fading of particles are merely forms of motion of the field".

Thirring was careful to put quotes around the word "void". Space is not void; it is not empty. To the contrary, space is a dynamic fullness interrelated with other dimensional spaces and unified into one grand plenum.

The Chinese sage, Chang Tsai, said it this way:

"When one knows that the great void is full of chi (energy) one realizes that there is no such thing as nothingness."

The dominant force in the field, at a specific time, determines the nature of the field. Gravity, for instance, is the dominant force on earthly bodies, thus, the gravitational field exerts itself as weight.

When astronauts leave the gravitational field of the earth the dominant forces change. In space, the pull of gravity is absent; they experience weightlessness. The dominant force becomes electromagnetic. Thus, the electromagnetic field exerts itself as heat, light, radiowaves, etc.

The pendulumist must be aware of the dominant force in a field at any given moment in order to tune accurately to a frequency or frequencies.

Let's say you want to ask a question. You hold the pendulum and ask. A heavy metal rock band is blasting through a stereo speaker.

Your accuracy, unless you are a master pendulumist, will be suspect. The dominant sound of rock music most likely will interfere with your auric field. Attention, thought, emotion and feeling may become unsteady.

To the degree that your psychological forces are disturbed at any moment determines the quality and accuracy of your tuning, reception and answer.

With the pendulum the unknown can become known. You become a cosmic explorer. Your consciousness can travel to new dimensions. Secrets are revealed and treasures are found.

The invisible fields, forces and frequencies can be touched, felt and experienced as easily as the book you are now holding, touching, feeling and experiencing.

Now to the nitty-gritty, the how-to, the simple at first and then complex step by step process of learning.

SUMMARY

1. Sound, light, thought and love - every person, place and thing, the invisible and the visible - All That Is- vibrates at a specific frequency.

2. Using the pendulum, you can explore the infinite, multi-dimensional energy world. You can tune-in to the invisible thousands of miles away or the visible right where you are.

3. When you become conscious in the frequency world all-knowing becomes available to you. You simply tune-in to the frequency or frequencies and you register, experience and know.

4. **You** and **no one else** can cultivate the physical repose, emotional calm, peace of mind and focused tuning necessary to become a pendulumist.

5. In the energy world there are four forces. A force is energy in motion following a fixed, repetitious pattern.

6. On an everyday physical/sensation level we all experience the four forces as fire, air, water and earth.

7. The Gnostic-Alchemist observed the activity and effects of the four forces and learned about the structure and order of the cosmos.

8. A Gnostic-Alchemist is one who knows the way, goes the way and experiences the transmutation of base sense, emotion, desire and thought into the light of wisdom and love.

9. The Alchemist, the Gnostic, the initiate who harnesses the four forces of his psychic nature becomes a reflector of "higher force". A kind of etheric presence is felt as peace, perception and strength all at once.

10. Your knowledge and harnessing of the inner psychological forces of spirit-fire, thought-air, water-feeling and earth- sensation is,perhaps, 75% of mastering the pendulum.

11. We are surrounded, interpenetrated, integrated and sustained by the universal field.

12. The pendulumist must be aware of the dominant force in a field at any given moment in order to tune accurately to a frequency or frequencies.

13. The invisible fields, forces and frequencies can be touched, felt and experienced as easily as the book you are now holding, touching, feeling and experiencing.

CHAPTER 4: HOW TO USE THE PENDULUM

The spring sun rayed its warmth through the window of a westside Manhattan apartment. The people inside, each in their own way, drank the solar rays as they listened to a lecture about how to use the pendulum.

Karl's words mingled with the sunlight as they found their way to the minds of the eager students.

"Does everyone have a pendulum?"

Sue spoke up with a tone of disappointment, "no...no, I don't have one. I wasn't here last week and I forgot to ask someone if there was any assignment."

"That's alright," Karl said in his usual understanding way. "Do you have a ring on one of your fingers?"

"Sure," replied Sue with a puzzled look on her face.

"Well, then you'll have your pendulum made in a matter of minutes." Karl turned to his wife, Laura, and asked her to bring him a piece of fishing line from his workroom.

Meanwhile the rest of the students wrestled their homemade pendulums from pockets, purses and briefcases. They buzzed, laughed and played, each showing off his or her creation. There were small ones and large ones, colorful ones and drab looking ones, strong ones and delicate ones but all with a basic form - a weight on the end of a string.

Laura returned with the fishing line.

"Thank you honey. Now, Sue bring me your ring and you'll have your pendulum in an instant." Sue handed Karl the gold band and remained standing next to him as he tied the line to the ring. "Here you go. That should be enough weight." He held the makeshift pendulum out in front of him to test the weight. Satisfied with the balance as well as the weight, he handed it to Sue.

"Okay everybody."

Silence returned to the room.

"The first thing you have to do is program your subconscious. Everyone take out a sheet of paper."

A symphony of rubbing, turning and ripping followed.

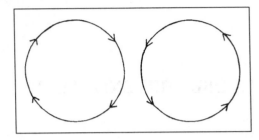

Figure 3: Circles that illustrate pendulum motion.

"Now, draw two circles close to each other, as round as possible. There are three compasses on the coffee table if you're like me and your free hand circles tend to look like blobs." (see Figure 3 to the left).

"Circles drawn?" Karl looked around the room. Sue was the last to finish her circles. "Now, before we get to the circles, draw a verticle line crossed by a horizontal line below the circles."

Karl smiled. His students had an assortment of puzzled looks on their faces. (see Figure 4 on the next page).

Jim raised his hand. Karl acknowledged him with a nod of the head.

"What's this all about Karl? - these circles and lines?"

A couple of yeahs went off from the others, backing Jim's question.

"Hey you guys, give me a chance," said Karl still with the smile on his face. "Before we get to the circles and lines I have to show you how to hold your pendulums." A few groans followed. "Are there any lefthanders in the room?" Betty raised her hand. "Alright, Betty naturally you'll hold the pendulum in your left hand, grasping the string between the thumb and index finger." Karl demonstrated the proper holding of the pendulum in the left hand while facing in Betty's direction. She sat next to the television-radio-stereo console on the side of the room opposite Jim and next to Sue.

"The rest of you righthanders hold the pendulum like this." He switched hands. Everyone now held a pendulum.

"How long should the string be?" spoke up Bill. All laughed because Bill had about 10 inches of string between his fingers and the top of the pendulum.

"Don't laugh," admonished Karl in a joking tone. The length of the string should be whatever feels natural to you. I find for myself that about three to five inches is the best. A number of pendulum books give complicated formulas for finding the exact length of string. I find them tedious and unnecessary. "Bill, if you find 10 inches of string comfortable, then that's right for you."

"Karl, I don't think there's enough string on this one for me," said Bill with a clowning expression. Again the whole class roared. Karl and Laura laughed as well. Everybody held their pendulum at the longest length of string possible.

The class settled down, returning their attention to Karl. Everyone was eager to find out the answers to some pressing questions.

"Now, before we can receive any answers from the pendulum, we must explore the pendulum's movements and then program our subconscious. I want everyone to sit up straight and have both feet flat on the floor," reminded Karl.

"Why is that so important?" asked Bill. "Is it not more important to be relaxed and comfortable?"

"For one thing Bill you tend to get a better flow of energy through the nervous system when sitting upright. For another your powers of concentration are better sitting up than they are when you're slouching. Also, you're right about being relaxed and comfortable, but you can be relaxed while sitting upright just as well as when you're lying down."

Karl turned his attention to the class. "In fact, while you hold the pendulum, be sure you're as loose as possible. Don't hold your arm stiff. Let the tensions go from your shoulder and back muscles. Everybody take some deep breaths, perhaps four or five. Karl paused while everyone loosened up and did the breathing.

"Okay, let's see if your minds can influence matter," suggested Karl with a slight smile.

"You mean like mind over matter." piped up Betty.

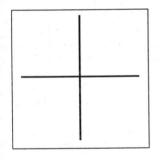

Figure 4: Axis for pendulum positioning.

"That's right. Everybody get your pendulum precisely over the axis point of the two lines. (See Figure 4 to the left). Concentrate your mind force on the pendulum and will it to move along the vertical line. Don't move it yourself. Will it to move with your mind."

The class was perfectly silent. Everyone concentrated. Pendulums began moving, some slowly and some rapidly. A few of the young people were amazed, letting out gasps, ooo's and aaa's. No one could deny that the pendulum was moving by no other means than by the will of their mind.

"Now, using the power of your mind, make the pendulum come to a stop at the center point of the axis." Again the students were amazed at the response. Karl continued giving directions. "Next, move the pendulum along the horizontal line. Once you have it going, bring it to a halt at the center point always using your mental energies."

All were able to complete the mind over matter experiment except Carol. The frustration on her face signaled Karl to ask her, "are you having any problems Carol?"

"It doesn't want to move for me. I can't understand it. Everyone else seems to have success except me." A feeling of defeat was in her eyes.

"Let's try to find the source of the difficulty," declared Karl confidently. "First of all, what's your attitude about the possibility of mind over matter?

"Very, very sceptical," answered Carol almost curtly.

"That may be our problem Carol."

"How so?"

"Our attitudes are part of our subconscious mind. Now, if the force of your scepticism is stronger than the force of your conscious effort to move the pendulum then the chances of it moving are wiped out."

"What can I do to change my attitude?"

"For one thing stop identifying with it. Let it go. Take the neutral attitude of a scientist, you're not for or against. Just see what happens."

Carol tried again. But still with no success. The whole class was watching her this time and she felt overly self-conscious.

"If I'm not mistaken, this time the class watching you is making you self-conscious," said Karl with understanding.

"That's true." agreed Carol.

"Then I would suggest that you practice at home on your own. The self-consciousness here takes away from your concentration. A few more tries, doing as I have suggested, and you'll have it."

"How about the circles," asked Jim eagerly. "What are they for?"

"Alright Jim," acknowledged Karl, "the circles will help you program our subconscious as to the meaning of the pendulum's movements." Karl's eyes scanned the class. (See Figure 3, page 26.) "Hold your pendulum over the circle on the left. Will the pendulum again with your mind-force to move in a clockwise rotation around the circle. At the same time talk to your subconscious silently or out loud saying, 'a clockwise rotation means yes'. Say it at least three times while watching your pendulum rotate. Doing this should make the message to your subconscious clear."

Karl, whined Carol, "my pendulum is not moving again." The rest of the class went ahead with the instructions while Karl turned his attention to Carol.

"In that case Carol, start moving the pendulum with your hand."

"But will my subconscious get the message?"

"As long as you talk to your subconscious and see the clockwise rotation the message should be clear enough."

Reluctantly, Carol followed Karl's instructions. The look on her face showed dissatisfaction but Karl knew that her subconscious would be programmed clearly.

Turning to the class, Karl continued with his instruction. "Now repeat the same steps holding the pendulum over the other circle only this time the pendulum should turn counterclockwise. (See Figure 3, page 26.) This time tell your subconscious 'a counter-clockwise rotation means no'."

The entire class went about their training eagerly. Everyone was becoming a bit anxious about really using the pendulum to find answers to some pressing problems in business, in relationships and in the emotional life.

Carol had little difficulty this time around using the alternate method. Bill finished quickly and started clowning by spinning his pendulum wildly. Sue used her ring pendulum without a hitch. Betty, on the other hand, followed the instructions alright but felt a little awkward. Being a lefty she felt like doing everything the opposite of the righthanders.

"Doing it the way you said Karl makes me feel uncomfortable," declared Betty. "Could it be that being a lefty makes a difference?"

"It could be. Your subconscious may already be programmed to do a lot of things opposite to how righthanders go about it. I'll tell you what, let me ask my pendulum whether or not it would be wise for you to program your subconscious with counterclockwise meaning 'yes' and clockwise meaning 'no'."

As Karl spoke he pulled out his pendulum and held it out in front of him. The entire class was listening and watching now. This was the first practical use of the pendulum they would see. The pendulum began moving clockwise, for Karl a yes answer.

"Alright, Betty, it looks as if your feeling was accurate. In your case it is better to program your subconscious counterclockwise meaning 'yes' and clockwise meaning 'no'."

"Okay, I'll go ahead and do the programming on my own. I don't want to hold up the rest of the class."

"Thank you, Betty, but there's another important point I'm reminded of by where you're sitting." The class looked at Betty's chair.

"Don't tell us Karl. Betty's chair is a lefthand pendulum user's chair." joked Bill. Needless to say, the class roared with laughter.

"No Bill, not quite. It's the television-radio-stereo console. Using the pendulum around high voltage electrical equipment tends to throw off your readings. Their powerful radiations may cause the pendulum to gyrate wildly giving you a difficult time getting a correct answer. In fact, Betty, maybe it would be wise for you to program your subconscious away from the television."

"But it is not turned on right now," challenged Betty.

"Still, the fact remains, it has been on recently. Some of the vibrations from the television images may still be lingering around the set. You know what junk is on the tube these days; so you can imagine the quality of the vibrations around the set."

Jim had been sitting quietly to this point following all the instructions to the letter. But now his eagerness to get on with some practical uses of the pendulum prompted him to speak up.

"When are we going to get down to business? How do we use this thing to find out some answers to our pressing life problems?"

"Before we can answer some of the more important questions in the areas of health, relationships and business," Karl said in a cautious tone, "we must begin with easy experiments. You cannot expect to get 100% accurate answers in the beginning."

"What kind of experiments?" asked Jim still eager to get on with the learning process.

Karl picked up an apple from the table in front of him. "Let's start with this."

"You mean we have to eat an apple to be a good pendulumist," quipped Bill.

"No, not at all," Karl said chuckling. "Here Bill." Karl handed the apple to Bill. "Put the apple on the table in front of you with the stem end up. Hold your pendulum over the end of the apple."

"Like this?" Bill held his pendulum over the apple.

"Not quite," replied Karl quickly. "Remember what I said earlier Bill?"

"Oh, yes about sitting up."

"Right. Remember - sit with feet apart and firmly planted on the floor. Do not have your hands or legs crossed, or touching each other while doing a reading. Crossing your hands or legs tends to shortcircuit your tuning."

"How about Bill's attitude about the reading?" asked Carol remembering her difficulty.

"The attitude is vitally important. Bill, as far as it is possible, remain mentally and emotionally neutral about the outcome of the reading. Have no opinion about the outcome. Simply hold the pendulum over the apple and see what happens."

Following instructions to the best of his ability, Bill held the pendulum over the stem end of the apple. He noticed as he tried to be mentally neutral that a few thoughts popped into his head out of nowhere. Instead of giving them his attention and energy he let them go. Remaining as neutral as possible, the pendulum began to slowly move in a clockwise rotation.

"It seems the pendulum is telling us that the stem end of this particular apple has a positive charge," said Bill with caution.

"That's right," Karl agreed, "now turn the apple over and check the opposite end. Be sure to remain neutral. Do not try to anticipate the answer. If you see yourself mentally or emotionally anticipating take a few slow deep breaths through the nose."

Bill turned the apple over and again followed the steps laid out by Karl. Slowly the pendulum began to rotate in a counterclockwise direction indicating a negative polarity.

"I really feel something," declared Bill enthusiastically, "I actually feel a sort of vibration coming from the end of the apple. A kind of flow of energy between the apple and the pendulum."

"You got it Bill. Remember from your physics class everything in the so called physical universe is made up of energy. It's simple. You are tuning-in to the energy system of the apple giving you a first hand experience of its vitality, its life."

"Sure Karl, what you say sounds logical enough," challenged Jim, "but how do you know what you say is true?"

"Don't take my word for it or Bill's word for it. Try it yourself. Karl walked over to the table in front of Bill and picked up the apple and then, stepping to Jim's seat handed the apple to him. "Here you go, give it a try. Let's see what you get."

Jim proceeded to repeat the apple experiment with the same results. He too felt the energy connection between the apple and his hand.

"Are you satisfied now Jim?" inquired Karl.

"I have no doubt. It does work. What other experiments can we do?"

"There's another one along the same lines as the apple experiment. Everybody pair off." Bill and Sue got together while Jim and Betty became partners. Carol was left so Karl worked with her.

"Come on Sue, let's dance." Bill took Sue by the hand and tried to get her to stand up. "Come on Sue we can swing like the pendulum."

"Don't fool around Bill. These experiments are serious," Sue said adamantly.

"Let Bill clown, Sue," interjected Karl, "I think it helps him to relax."

"Alright, but I don't want to dance," reasserted Sue.

Bill will have to take your hand in this experiment but you don't have to dance." Wonder spread across the faces of the five students. "I see you can't imagine what's next. Carol, let's start with you. Hold your pendulum over the palm of my right hand."

The class was silent, allowing Carol to bring her concentration to a single point. Following the steps she learned in the apple experiment, Carol placed both feet flat on the floor, sat upright in a relaxed position, took three or four breaths and remained as neutral as possible. Remarkably the pendulum began to gyrate in a clockwise direction almost instantly.

"It works. I feel the energy connection with your hand. I think the pendulum and I are starting to get along."

"Now check my left hand," instructed Karl.

Carol repeated the same steps over Karl's left hand. This time the pendulum rotated in a circular counterclockwise direction.

Bill and Sue as well as Jim and Betty, got on with their hand experiment. Bill, Sue and Betty had no difficulty coming up with the same results as Carol. Jim's results proved to be puzzling. He could not understand why the pendulum swung counterclockwise over Betty's right hand and clockwise over her left hand.

"Say Karl," said Jim with a bit of hesitation in his voice, "what's going on? I think my pendulum is going haywire." Betty just smiled.

"Have you thought of all the factors in your experiment Jim?"

"Let's see. I sat up straight, did the breathing..." Jim paused thinking to himself. Then a flash of intuition crossed his face bringing a knowing expression. "Betty is lefthanded."

"You got it right," agreed Karl.

"The pendulum then seems to detect polarities," interjected Betty.

"That's right Betty. Both the apple and hand experiments had to do with the measurement of positive and negative energies. We did not ask the pendulum a yes/no question. By simply holding it over an object we determined the positive and negative poles."

"You mean everything has a positive and negative pole?" asked Sue in disbelief.

"I'll put it this way," said Karl being careful not to be dogmatic, "the earth has a north pole and a south pole; an atom has a proton and an electron. Try to discover something which does not have polarity."

"Let's ask some yes/no questions," Bill suggested eagerly.

"Yeah," seconded Jim, "I want to find out some answers to some of my pressing problems."

"Wait a moment Jim. Hold your horses. You must work by degrees. The learning process cannot be rushed. First you must master simple yes/no questions. Then, as your skill with the pendulum improves, graduate to the more pressing yes/no questions."

"What kind of questions should we start with?" probed Jim.

"At first we want to stick with questions which we can find the answers to immediately. In other words, answers we can verify with our senses. Here's a good one to start with. Do I have at this time a $5.00 bill in my pocket?"

"Would it be easier for us to get a correct answer if we hold the pendulum over one of the circles?" asked Sue.

"Perhaps, visualizing the circle may set up a better reception line with the subconscious but remember we have already programmed our subconscious computer so it is not necessary to use the circles."

Everyone sat up straight holding their pendulum out in front. If someone had walked into the room at that moment who could say how they would react. Maybe he would think they were in training to become clocks; not ordinary clocks but coo-coo clocks.

"Who got a yes answer?" Bill, Betty and Sue raised their hands. "Then I assume Jim and Carol received a no answer?"

"I got a no answer," affirmed Jim.

"And Carol, how about you?"

"I'm back to my troubles again. It's difficult trying to stay in neutral. For one thing I was uptight about getting the correct answer."

"Did you do the breathing," asked Karl.

"Sure, I took four or five deep breaths."

"Instead of stopping at four or five breaths continue slow rhythmic breathing throughout the reading. Go ahead. See what answer you get."

"I'll try it," Carol said with hesitation. This time she kept the breathing up. The pendulum rotated in a clockwise circle - yes.

Karl laughed as he looked at Jim. "It looks like you're the odd man out. Four to one in favor that I have a $5.00 bill.

"What went wrong?" asked Jim with emotion.

"Take it easy Jim. Rome was not built in a day. Remember what I said about steps. Learning how to use the pendulum with skill and a high degree of accuracy cannot be done on the first day. Becoming a carpenter, a dentist, a computer programmer is a training requiring time, energy, practice and an ability to learn from your mistakes and failures. Everyone in this room will make mistakes along the way toward becoming a skilled pendulumist. That's one of the reasons I want you to begin with simple yes/no questions which can be verified quickly. By checking your result immediately you can see just how well you are doing. Eventually, as your accuracy increases to 80% plus, more important questions can be answered accurately."

"Okay Karl. What you say makes sense. Still, I would like to know what went wrong."

"What were your subconscious attitudes while doing the reading? Were you afraid you would make a mistake? Were you overeager? You must remain as mentally-emotionally neutral as possible."

"I'm not sure."

"So, then, in the next readings try to notice what is blocking the pendulum's clear channel."

"Let's try another question," Carol asked now that she had a little more confidence.

"Alright, here's another one for you. Remember, as I have said before, remain as neutral as possible. Do we have more than a quart of milk in the refrigerator at this time?"

Everybody held out their pendulum following the proper steps. Carol continued using the slow breathing that helped bring her last success. Jim seemed to be a little more cautious this time, wanting to remain as neutral as possible. Bill's and Sue's pendulums rotated counterclockwise, a no answer.

Betty's and Carol's answers were just the opposite, a yes answer. Oddly enough, Jim's pendulum did not gyrate in either direction.

"How can that be Karl? My pendulum did not want to rotate at all."

"Don't worry about it Jim. Let's find out firsthand just how much milk is in the refrigerator. Perhaps, then, we will understand your seemingly peculiar lack of gyration."

Everyone sprung from their seats not wanting to lose a second to see which answer was the correct one. Karl and Laura led the way to the kitchen.

"Would you like to do the honors honey?" asked Karl of his wife with a sense of drama.

Standing in front of the refrigerator with her hand grasping the handle Laura paused, building the suspense. Then, in a jerk, the door opened. All eyes scanned the contents. There was not a drop to be seen.

"Why did you trick us Karl? What are you trying to become Merlin the Magician?" quipped Bill.

"Yeah, that's not fair," agreed Betty "you knew all along there was no milk in the refrigerator."

"Take it easy, alright, alright." These words calmed the storm of talk. "Think about it for a second. Didn't we learn something more about how important it is to remain neutral?"

"That's right," Betty bellowed. "Even our attitude that every answer has to be either yes or no prevents us from staying in neutral."

"You hit the nail on the head Betty. I warned you all before I gave you the question to remain as neutral as possible. In fact, I sort of overemphasized it with the tone of my voice which could have been a dead giveaway."

"You did not fool me Karl," Jim said proudly.

"It looks like the tables were turned this time Jim, four incorrect answers against your lone correct answer. But be careful. You do not want to be overconfident or too proud. It could throw off your next pendulum reading. Why don't we go back into the living room."

Everyone headed back into their seats except Laura who stayed behind to fix a plate of snacks. By the time everyone settled down Laura returned with some carob cookies and a carrot cake. Bill was the first to dig in with the others right after him.

"Not bad." complimented Bill, "where did you get the recipe?"

"My mother gave it to me the last time she visited."

"I'd like to know how to make the carrot cake," requested Sue.

"I'll give you the recipe before you leave," volunteered Laura.

"Mentioning your mother Laura gives me an idea for another pendulum question. Here's a question that will bring us to the next step in our lesson. 'Is Laura's mother coming to visit us'? But wait. Before you pick up your pendulums, think. Is it an intelligent question?"

There was a pause. Carol raised her hand first.

"The question is too vague. Undoubtedly your mother-in-law will come to visit you sometime. The way it is worded now is meaningless. You don't need a pendulum to answer it."

"How should the question be worded?" asked Karl of the class.

"The question should be more specific," suggested Bill.

"I know, blurted out Betty, "we should ask the question in terms of time. Is Laura's mother coming in one week, two weeks, three weeks and so on until the pendulum gives a yes answer."

"Excellent Betty. In fact, the art of using the pendulum depends to a great degree on asking intelligent yes/no questions. The key seems to be setting limits that make sense. Betty's suggestion that we set limits of time is a good example. Using Betty's question, let's see what answer we receive."

Sue's and Bill's pendulums gave a yes answer at one week. Carol and Jim got a yes at two weeks. Betty's pendulum said no at both one and two weeks. She tried again and received a yes for both. On her own she reworded the question to be even more specific asking successively one week one day, one week two days, etc. Using this more exact questioning process Betty's pendulum gave a clockwise rotation on ten days. Everyone reported their answer to Karl.

"I guess no one had a wrong answer this time. We did not get specific enough. Betty used more precise limits getting ten days. Laura, when is your mother coming to visit?"

"In ten days according to what she told me on the phone last night. But when she said it her voice tone suggested a give or take of a couple days."

"That may explain the different readings."

"What do you mean Karl?" asked Jim.

"Laura's mother may not have an exact precise time in mind. Instead, her subconscious is toying with different times ranging from one week to two weeks."

"I can see how you ask the question is really important," Sue interjected.

"In fact, the art of using the pendulum is in many ways the art of wording the question. You must ask intelligent questions. For example, to ask "is Bill's brother alright?" is a nonsense question."

"Why?" joked Bill.

"For one thing we do not know if you have a brother or not. And if you do have a brother what do we mean by the word "alright"? We must have, as much as possible, clear and specific referents for our words. If we mean alright physically, we should ask it as part of the question. If we mean mentally, emotionally or financially, we must state it as part of the question."

"What other tips can you give us about wording our questions?" inquired Jim.

"Be careful of nonsense questions. For example, if you ask "will I ever marry"? knowing you are completely against marriage is a pointless question.

The pendulum will obviously give you a negative answer. Yet another area of questioning you should especially be wary of at the beginning of your training is questions about the future. The future is plastic, ever being molded by your thoughts, feelings and actions in the present. You will probably not get very good results on future questions until you have fairly good control of your thoughts, feelings and actions in the present."

"Anything else?" asked Betty.

"Not for now. I think we have had quite a dose for an introductory lesson. That's it for today."

SUMMARY

1. Hold the pendulum between the thumb and index finger. Let the string hang at a comfortable length.

2. When doing readings sit up straight with both feet flat on the floor. You tend to get a better flow of energy through the nervous system when sitting up.

3. Be as relaxed as possible. Let the tensions go from your arm, shoulder and back muscles. Take 4 or 5 deep breaths.

4. Use the circles to help you program your subconscious to the meaning of the pendulum's movements.

5. Hold the pendulum over the clockwise circle. Will the pendulum with your mind force to move in a clockwise rotation around the circle. At the same time talk to your subconscious silently or outloud saying "a clockwise rotation means yes". Say it at least three times while watching your pendulum rotate. Repeat process for no - the counterclockwise rotation.

6. Be aware of the atmosphere and environment you're in while doing readings. Are there negative vibrations or a lot of electrical equipment, etc.

7. Before you can answer some of the more important questions in the areas of health, relationships and business you must begin with easy experiments. You cannot expect to get 100% accurate answers in the beginning.

8. As far as it is possible, remain mentally and emotionally neutral about the outcome of the reading. Have no opinion about the outcome.

9. You must learn by degrees. First, you must master simple yes/no questions. Then, as your skill with the pendulum improves, graduate to the more pressing yes/no questions.

10. Watch your mental-emotional attitudes. Assuming every question has a clear yes or no answer may prevent you from staying in neutral.

11. The art of using the pendulum is in many ways the art of wording the questions. You must ask specific questions. Vaguely worded questions are meaningless.

12. Be wary of questions about the future. The future is plastic, ever being molded by your thoughts, feelings, and actions in the present. You will probably not get very good results on future questions until you have fairly good control of your thoughts, feelings and actions in the present.

CHAPTER 5: SEMANTIC PENDULUM

Verbal Maps

All of us have had the experience of asking for directions while driving in an unfamiliar town. Usually you will stop at a service station and ask the attendant where such and such a street is.

One of three things usually happens. The attendant says he knows the street you're looking for and gives you directions like: go two blocks, take a left at the light, then a quick right. Go one mile until you see Blank Road. Turn onto Blank Road until you get to such and such a street.

Invariably you get lost again. The directions are unclear. The attendant's verbal map does not fit the territory. He tried to steer you in the right direction. Some of the directions checked out. But he usually leaves out key landmarks which would benefit you immensely. The attendant forgets you have never driven that route before whereas he may have been over it a thousand times.

The second thing that often happens is the attendant plain gives you the wrong directions. He may have misunderstood you or, as often is the case, they make a habit of sending tourists on wild goose chases. In this instance the verbal map is nothing more than a meaningless noise.

The third possibility has a happy ending. The attendant gives you clear, concise, accurate directions. Usually, you're fairly close to your destination so he only needs to mention three or four direction changes. His verbal map reflects the actual territory.

Let's label these three possibilities:

1. The fuzzy verbal map.
2. The verbal map noise.
3. The accurate verbal map.

When I, you or anyone speaks or writes, one of these three comes into play. It is critical that we be aware of which level you or another is coming from when speaking or writing. If you are mistaking verbal map noises for accurate verbal maps then frustration, anger, hatred and suffering may very well be the result.

On the other hand, if you take accurate verbal maps to be verbal map noises then again frustration, anger, hatred and suffering may result. Of course, if you take a fuzzy verbal map for either a map noise or an accurate map you're still headed for trouble.

Practice becoming more aware of verbal maps. Listen to the radio and television. Read newspapers and magazines. Listen to yourself and to others. Differentiate, perceive precisely the clarity of the verbal maps. See if you can distinguish which verbal maps are fuzzy, which are noises and which are accurate. Notice how often you really know for sure.

If you are not sure say to yourself 'insufficient data'. In other words it may or may not be accurate, a noise or fuzzy but you do not know for sure. You have to check it out to be relatively sure.

Why the hairsplitting? Because when asking the pendulum a question an accurate answer depends a great deal on a clearly worded question. A fuzzy question, a fuzzy answer, a noise question, a meaningless answer. An accurate question, a clear answer.

A pendulumist must cultivate a keen awareness regarding the quality of a verbal map. Part of developing a tuning-in skill with the pendulum requires training your awareness of verbal map accuracy in everyday life.

Again, while going about your day listen more attentively, read more acutely. Can you sense the degree of accuracy? Keep practicing. Your ability in sensing verbal map accuracy will increase your accuracy with the pendulum by at least 50%.

Why General Semantics?

In 1933 a polish engineer and mathematician, Alfred Korzybski, published **Science and Sanity**, the source book of "General Semantics". Korzybski used the word "general" before the word semantics to avoid identifications with the study of words, semantics. General Semantics is much broader; it is the application of the methods, habits and viewpoints of science to the everyday problems of living.

Korzybski observed men, women, and cultures through the eyes of an engineer. He observed the structure, function and order of individual men and women and culture as-a-whole.

He saw that humans are not animals. He realized it was a grave error for humans to assume they were part animal. He saw how this ingrained belief was greatly responsible for the "survival of the fittest," "dog eat dog" mentality between people, businesses and countries.

He saw that humans were structured differently than animals. That difference he called his timebinding theory: humans pass on to each other what they have learned; each one starts where his predecessors ended.

Animals, on the other hand, repeat the same survival patterns as the generations before. Birds, for instance, build their nest today in much the same way as they did thousands of years ago. Humans, on the other hand, build elaborate homes, and condominiums and apartment buildings. We do not live in huts and teepees like our ancestors.

Our food, clothing and shelter, everything we have, is dependent upon the efforts of those who came before. And those who come after us are dependent on our efforts. Thus, Korzybski concluded: humans bind time and are bound together in time.

Realizing humans were structured differently than animals, Korzybski knew humans must function differently than animals. He observed that scientists were among the most efficient human timebinders. He asked himself, what do scientists do that most of the rest of us don't do? He concluded that scientists revise their premises when they no longer fit the facts.

Non-scientists, the majority of the rest of the population, tended to cling to rigid viewpoints, premises, attitudes and behaviors. This tendency Korzybski pointed out was "copying animals in our nervous response". To counteract this non-survival pattern for humans he suggested we each use the methods of science in our day to day living.

Scientists formulate theories, ideas about how the world works. Then they observe how the world works. If the actual process on the non-verbal level is different than the formulated theory (remember the verbal maps?) then the scientist modifys his theory.

Most of us do not apply this fundamental scientific method to daily life. We all tend to hold certain theories, ideas, attitudes, beliefs, faiths, views, philosophies, concepts, etc., etc. (verbal maps) as right, good, our philosophy, what we believe, etc., without checking it out against the process level - reality. Consequently, we non-scientists are constantly having "problems".

A scientific pendulumist must apply the scientific method of observing non-verbal energy structures, functions and orders and then asking questions (verbal map questions) that are accurate to the reality (the process level). This means remaining receptive to new facts. If you become aware of a new aspect to the question or situation at hand, the scientific pendulumist modifies his question accordingly.

Asking Specific Questions

So many times over the years people have asked me to do a pendulum reading without having their questions clearly stated. Often their verbal map questions are fuzzy or noisy.

Here are just a few of the typical vague questions. Does so and so love me? Am I healthy? Will I be rich? Has Johnny been a good boy? Where should I go on my vacation?

Do you see why these questions are vague? In General Semantics Korzybski pointed out the difference between high order abstractions and low order abstractions. For instance, in the question "has Johnny been a good boy?" The word good is a high order abstraction. What does the questioner mean specifically by the word "good"?

More often than not I must ask questions of the person who requested the reading before I can formulate a specific question. I might ask the client, "what do you mean by "good"? What is it specifically you want to know?"

Sometimes they get hung-up on their original word "good". They may or may not know what they mean by "good" so I must be patient in trying to discover the underlying specific question.

I might explain to them that "good" can mean almost anything to anybody. One person's "good" might be another person's "bad". It's relative to a person's value system.

One parent might consider Johnny's musical talent "good", another might consider it "bad"! One parent sees the joy on Johnny's face when he plays piano. Another parent cowers at the joy believing "all musicians are trouble"; "they can't make a living," etc.

Now, if I can give the client specific examples of what I mean perhaps they can give me specific examples of what they mean when they ask, "is Johnny a good boy"? Hopefully, the client will recall specific instances of Johnny's behavior or possible behavior. The client may ask, more specifically, "is Johnny eating too many cookies"?

Now we are getting somewhere. This question is still not specific enough for my taste but it helps me to formulate the final question: "Is Johnny eating too many cookies relative to his dietary needs?"

Did you catch the fuzzy verbal map, the high order abstraction: "Too many" for one person is "too little" or "just enough" for others.

The concerned parent who asked me about her son's cookie habit had her suspicions confirmed: yes, Johnny was eating too many cookies for his dietary needs. This answer led to many more specific questions about why he craved cookies and what could be done to cut down his cookie intake.

Holding the pendulum comfortably in an attentive, calm and relaxed mental-emotional-physical state is certainly important for achieving accurate pendulum readings, but pendulum accuracy depends just as much on Asking Specific Questions, **Master Key #1**.

The concerned mother began by asking: (1) Is Johnny a good boy? That verbal map noise, the question was essentially meaningless, evolved into: (2) Is Johnny eating too many cookies? We were getting there but we still had a fuzzy verbal map question. By wording the question even more specifically,

(3) Is Johnny eating too many cookies for his dietary needs? we finally came closer to an accurate verbal map question.

As Korzybski so perceptively saw, the more accurate the verbal map matches the structure of reality, the better we can interact with people, places and things. This fundamental fact when applied to the pendulum, asking specific questions, leads the novice pendulumist to becoming the intermediate pendulumist.

Diligent effort along the lines outlined here will pay off dramatically. Your accuracy will improve rapidly. The pendulum will respond more quickly. The pendulum's movements will be accompanied by distinct feelings, clear thoughts and precise verbal maps for describing your answers.

When Indexing

Have you ever eaten half a banana and put the other half aside? I suspect you have at one time or another; or at least known someone who has.

When you pick up the ripe banana the skin is predominantly yellow. You peal back the skin and eat part of the banana. You set the other half, still in the peel, on the counter.

An hour later you come into the kitchen. You notice the banana. What do you see? The yellow peel has turned brown to black. The banana at 9:00 is not the same banana at 10:00.

Ralph Waldo Emerson put it succinctly "The world rolls; the circumstances vary every hour." The only constant in life is change. A pendulumist must be aware of changes in people, places and things.

When you ask a question, tune-in and receive an answer, you must remember that the answer you pick up on today is not necessarily going to be the same answer you will pick up on tomorrow. True, there may be some strong similarities but there might also be some vast differences.

Novice pendulumists would make a wise decision to date their answers, especially if you write the answers down.

If you keep a record of your answers or give written answers to friends the "*when indexing*" will remind you of changes. Eventually, as you graduate to more difficult questions and people hear of your skill they will come to you for answers.

After asking their question you can remind them that the answer picked up is for today, right now. Explain to them, everything changes. Life is dynamic; energy structures configurate, maintain and dissipate.

A friend called one day and asked me to come over that evening to see how the pendulum would respond to a few of her questions.

One of her questions illustrates the importance of "*when indexing*". She asked, "Is it wise for me to go into business with Bill Smith?" The pendulum rotated clockwise - yes. I felt a strong positive vibration; their life paths blended, at that time.

Bill had the capital and Carol had the product. They joined forces. Bill and Carol worked well together. Their business plans began to unfold.

Carol commented to me how accurate the pendulum was. I reminded her of when indexing. Yes, as of September 21, 1983 Bill and Carol were compatible business partners. Carol's experience verified that reading.

Several months went by. Their budding business hit some roadblocks. Bill's liquid capital dried up. Tensions mounted between them. A lot of "negative" events went down. Their partnership came to an abrupt ending.

She talked to me about their breakup. She said, "The pendulum picked up that we would be compatible business partners." Her voice tone revealed an attitude: the pendulum received a positive reading on September 21, 1983; it should be positive for all time.

The pendulum is not the Oracle of Delphi. **You** pick up **an** answer not **the** answer when you tune-in using the pendulum.

You, your friends, your students and your clients are responsible for what is happening. Be aware of the changes. Accept what is and adapt accordingly.

"When index" the answers you receive. Remind those you do readings for that the answer you are receiving today is not written in stone. Tomorrow is another day.

Usually before, during or after a reading suggest to the friend or client that they not swallow the answer whole. Look at their life circumstance. Check the reading against life-facts.

The pendulum is a helper not a god!

Semantic Reactions

"Sticks and stones will break my bones but words will never hurt me." My mother used to tell me this when some of the other kids in the neighborhood got nasty mouthed. When someone says something mean, it can hurt your feelings. That hurt you feel is a semantic reaction.

We all have trigger words. If someone calls us a certain name, uses lingo we don't understand, or discusses a topic not to our liking, we react emotionally.

Let me tell you a story to illustrate the point. A local business asked me to write a radio commercial. The word "Grandma" was used. It was definitely used in an uplifting, vital context, not in a condescending, you're-too-old context.

Once the commercial was produced and put on tape, I asked friends and family to listen to it. Everyone thought it was informative, attention getting and a touch humorous. Even the Marketing/Advertising Manager and his secretary thought it was done just right.

I left a cassette with the Marketing/Advertising Manager so the owners could listen to it for final approval. I called a couple days later. One of the four owners was a woman 60 years young. She did not like the word "Grandma".

Her emotional reaction to the verbal sound "Grandma" was one of her trigger words. Apparently, she was 60 and not a grandmother. It was a source of dissappointment for her. It seems her son had not married; at 40 he was a confirmed bachelor.

We changed the commercial to read "Aunt Bess" instead of "Grandma". Most everyone thought the commercial was less effective as a result. This multi-million dollar business ran the commercial across the Northwest United States.

In truth, words in and of themselves are totally meaningless. Without a context and a referent in life experience words are noises.

Wording specific questions requires awareness of your semantic reactions and the semantic reactions of those for whom you give readings. The masterful 20th century fiction writer, Ernest Hemingway, when asked why he got along so well with so many people from around the world answered "because I speak their language".

He did not mean he spoke every foreign language. He meant with fishermen he talked fishing, with scientists he talked science, with writers he talked writing, with soldiers he talked fighting, etc.

Knowing your trigger words and semantic reactions will help you in asking clear questions. Being aware of a friend's or client's verbal preference will assist you in wording the question without triggering a semantic reaction in your friend or client.

Emotional reactions, as you might expect, will throw off the reading. The interference vibration of negative emotion, more often than not, blocks the clear reception of the answer.

Your awareness of automatic reactions will serve you well when it comes to asking questions about your personal life - love, family, health and finances.

Many pendulumists have difficulty receiving accurate answers to their personal life questions. Personal likes, dislikes, desires, wants and rejections, especially when intensely powerful, can directly effect the pendulum's swing.

Practice, practice, practice, day in and day out becoming more and more aware of your trigger words, semantic reactions, emotional reactions, etc., then detach: stop feeding them energy. Gradually you will become more and more accurate tuning-in to your life, seeing and knowing answers to your questions.

Colloidal Behavior

"The term 'colloid' was first proposed in 1861 by British chemist Thomas Graham to describe the distinction between the behavior of those materials which readily crystallize and diffuse through animal membranes and those which form 'amorphous' or gelantinous masses and do not diffuse readily or at all through animal membranes. Graham called the first class 'crystalloids' and the second 'colloids', from the Greek work for glue.

From **Science and Sanity**, Korzybski.

"Electrical currents generated by feeling-thinking (psychological) processes play over the surface areas of the colloidal structure of a physiological organism, altering and changing surface-tensions, according to the positive-negative reciprocal relations pertaining thereto. These energy currents may be set up by one's own semantic reactions, values, etc., or they may be registered from another, or from environmental influences, content of the racial consciousness, emotional fervor, etc. Those psychological semantic reactions we label love, courage, fortitude, etc. (positive), fear, worry, jealousy, envy, etc. (negative), may be considered factors affecting the surface tensions of colloidal structures."

From **Healing Technic**, Vitvan.

Here we have **Master Key #2.** (Master Key #1 was Asking Specific Questions). *Becoming conscious of the environmental - psychological forces sweeping back and forth over your body's colloidal electro-magnetic tension surface is a must if you expect to achieve a high degree of pendulum accuracy.*

Once you have a question formulated in specific terms it is time to neutralize, as far as possible, disturbing environmental-psychological forces.

Become aware of potentially disturbing environmental forces like microwaves, high voltage electricity, radio activity, electromagnetic frequencies, cigarette smoke, sound pollution, etc. Take steps to eliminate their influence before proceeding. Or, if you cannot eliminate their influence, reduce them as much as possible or move to another, more harmonious location for your readings.

Even more important than environmental forces are the psychological forces. Mental-emotional activities generate electrical currents across the colloidal surface.

By the way, the total area of colloidal surfaces in humans is staggering. An area the size of #5 buckshot with fine particles .00000025 cm. in diameter has a total surface area of nearly half an acre, about 22,000 sq. feet!

Ask yourself, "What am I thinking? What am I feeling? What mood am I in? Is my energy level high and stable? Are strong likes, dislikes, wants, desires or revulsions coming into play on the colloidal surfaces?" If the psychological forces are relatively quiet the colloidal surface tension will be relatively neutral and, thus, more sensitive and receptive to the frequency of the answers.

On the other hand, if you notice psychological disturbances, no matter how subtle, (remember how vast the colloidal surface is) take immediate steps to detach, stop identifying and let go of these interfering mental-emotional activities **both positive and negative.**

A neutral, detached attentive psychological state is the recommended condition before actually asking the question. Many psychological disturbances can be eliminated by slow rhythmic breathing through the nose, relaxing the neck, shoulder and back muscles, etc.

Questions where powerful semantic reactions are automatically invoked in your psyche may not be worth asking. The colloidal disturbance will probably block the clear reception of the answer. It may take you months, or even years, to eliminate powerful semantic reactions.

Fundamental transformations in your psychological nature must be affected through a long term commitment to self-knowledge, elimination of self-destructive patterns and service to others. Chapter 6 will be devoted to an overview of this transformation process.

"One's own functional development, state of consciousness or self-awareness, must be considered determinative as to what the effect (of registered forces or frequencies) may be. That is to say, to one whose own development and understanding enable him to protect himself, even destructive forces in the racial consciousness, of tremendous force and power, will not necessarily be destructive to him. In fact, wherever frequencies registered seem to be destructive, inharmonious, deleterious in any way that which becomes of paramount importance to each one will be his own semantic evaluation of the frequency - registration (conscious or/and unconscious). Therefore the energy force of our own semantic evaluations operative upon the vast colloidal electrical - tension surface may be said to be determinative."

From **Healing Technic**, Vitvan.

SUMMARY

1. Become more aware of verbal maps. Perceive precisely the clarity of verbal maps. See if you can distinguish which verbal maps are fuzzy, which are noises and which are accurate.

2. When asking the pendulum a question an accurate answer depends a great deal on a clearly worded question.

3. General Semantics is the application of the methods, habits and viewpoints of science to the everyday problems of living.

4. Scientists, Korzybski concluded, revised their premises when they no longer fit the facts. Most of us, as non-scientists, tend to hold on to cer-

tain pet theories, attitudes,beliefs, faiths, etc., even when the life-facts change. The result: non-scientists are constantly having problems.

5. The scientific pendulumist must apply the scientific method of observing non-verbal energy structures, functions and orders and then asking questions (verbal map questions) that are accurate to reality (the process level).

6. Holding the pendulum comfortably in an attentive, calm and relaxed mental-emotional state is certainly important for achieving accurate pendulum readings but pendulum accuracy depends just as much on **Asking Specific Questions, Master Key #1.**

7. Diligent effort along these lines will pay off dramatically; your accuracy will improve rapidly. The pendulum will respond more quickly. The pendulum's movements will be accompanied by distinct feelings, clear thoughts and precise verbal maps for describing your answers.

8. When you ask a question, tune-in and receive an answer, you must remember that the answer you pick up on today is not necessarily the same answer you will pick up on tomorrow. True, there may be some strong similarities but there might also be some vast differences.

9. Pendulumists would make a wise decision to date their answers. "*When indexing*" will remind you of changes.

10. The pendulum is not the Oracle of Delphi. **You** pick up **an** answer not **the** answer.

11. Usually before, during or after a reading I suggest to the friend or client that they not swallow the answer whole. Look at their life circumstances. Check the reading out against life-facts. The pendulum is a helper, not a god!

12. Wording specific questions requires awareness of your semantic reactions and the semantic reactions of those for whom you give readings.

13. Semantic reactions, as you might expect, throw off the reading. The interference vibration of negative emotion will, more often than not, block the clear reception of the answer.

14. Becoming conscious of the environmental-psychological forces sweeping over your body's electro-magnetic colloidal tension- surface is a must, if you expect to achieve a high degree of pendulum accuracy, **Master Key #2.**

15. Once you have a question formulated in specific terms it is time to neutralize, as far as possible, disturbing environmental- psychological forces.

16. A neutral, detached, attentive psychological state is the recommended condition before actually asking the question.

17. If you notice psychological disturbances, no matter how subtle, take immediate steps to detach, stop identifying and let go of interfering mental-emotional activities both positive and negative.

CHAPTER 6: THE WELL-ROUNDED PENDULUMIST

Conscious Pendulumist

What do I mean here by "conscious"? To be conscious is to be acutely aware. I do not mean automatic everyday consciousness. There's a car. I've got to go to work. I'm hungry.

The kind of consciousness I am referring to requires effort, holding your attention in a state of wordless awareness. When you are conscious, people places and things are more immediate, more alive, more dynamic.

Here is a consciousness raising exercise that can be applied to daily life activities. Take five to ten objects randomly from around your house or apartment and put them on a table. Sit down, Pick up one object; look at it without associations.

How long are you able to look at it without thinking, imaging, associating, drifting, etc., 5 seconds, 10 seconds, a minute or more? In a conscious state you see without thinking, without activity in the mental-field.

Let's say you have a rose quartz paperweight something like the one on my desk. I look at it. I do not want to journey off into the memory of how I bought it. Instead, I perceptively observe.

I see hues, shades, lighter and darker pinks. The colors are layered from outside to inside. I see an imperfect circular shape about 3/4" thick and 3" in diameter. The top is smoother and convex, the bottom is rougher and concave. It weighs about 8 oz. There are fine lines crisscrossing throughout the quartz. I notice patches and lines of white quartz interspersed here and there within the pink quartz. I feel a soothing, calming, peaceful vibration. I begin to see the crystalline pattern; the crisscrossing lines form proportionate quadrangular diamond shapes, etc., etc., etc.

I could easily go on for 15 or 20 minutes right now becoming conscious of the rose quartz paperweight on my desk. Becoming conscious is a journey into now, an adventure into the cosmic sea. In becoming conscious of the rose quartz, I barely scratched the surface. It is alive with teeming life energy.

Practice the consciousness raising exercise. It will build up your aware-ness muscle. It will become a priceless tool for improved living. People and places will be alive with activity. You will see what's in front of you; you will see to your sides; you will even see behind you. You will develop 360 degree spherical vision. You will be conscious.

You will become aware of how your "inner" thoughts, feelings, moods, desires and emotions are connected with the events you meet in daily life. You will discover that by changing the quality of your thoughts, feelings and desires that the quality of "outer" events will change.

Using the pendulum, you can check the percentage of time anyone is con-scious. What percentage of the time is so and so conscious? 90 to 100% If you get a no answer, a counterclockwise rotation, then drop down - 80 to 90%?. etc., until you receive a clockwise yes answer.

Checking your own consciousness percentage may or may not be difficult depending on how neutral you are. Perhaps a fellow pendulumist can check it for you. Remember - whatever answer you receive verify by life-facts. Ob-serve yourself. How much of the time are you really conscious?

Another consciousness training exercise that may tune you to the con-scious frequencies is: see, look, touch, and feel, say to every person, place and thing "this is conscious now".

The more conscious the pendulumist, the more likely he or she will pick up, detect, receive, feel, etc. the ultra-subtle frequencies that are tuned-in. The well-rounded pendulumist must be conscious. Unconsciousness, lack of awareness, is met with more unconsciousness. Using the pendulum is about becoming more conscious not less conscious.

The Wheel of Whole Living

Look at Figure 5 on page 53. The eight-spoked wheel of whole living sym-bolizes the many interrelated areas of life you and I experience.

Dividing the wheel into 8 sections is rather arbitrary on my part. It could be many more or fewer. The lines between sections should be taken lightly. No life areas are isolated or completely separated from any other.

For instance, mental is not completely separate from emotional. You may see an intellectual cut off from emotion to a certain extent. Still, reason is colored by feelings more or less. The two are interrelated.

Becoming and being a dynamic well-rounded pendulumist requires, demands taking a good look at yourself. Using the eight-spoked wheel diagram as a mirror, take a look.

Start with the "physical" arc. Can you sense-feel-experience-know where you are "physically" at any given moment? Are you body conscious?

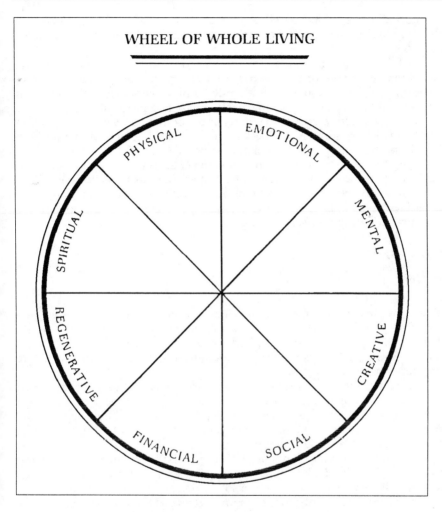

Figure 5: The Wheel of Whole Living.

Proceed to the "emotional" arc. Place your attention on this life energy. Do not analyse. It is not necessary. Simply look and see. All you want to do here is see where you are at now.

To be the well-rounded pendulumist you must first see where you are at now. You cannot drive from Los Angeles to San Francisco without knowing you are in Los Angeles in the first place.

Most all of us behave based on (1) reflection and (2) reaction. In each of the eight life areas we tend to be activated automatically by reflection and/or reaction.

There's a powerful tendency to absorb, reflect and react according to the environment you are in and the company you keep. Have you ever been to a sporting event? If you've ever attended a high school football game you know what I mean. Were you able to sit quietly and peacefully?

Now the question arises, do you really act or do you really re-act? Action without reaction is unusual. Check it out. We tend to react automatically to people, places, things, words, symbols, memories - the list is endless.

Begin becoming more conscious of your reflections and reactions in each of the eight life areas. The more aware you are of your reflections and reactions the more aware you will be of others' reflections and reactions. This awareness will improve the quality and preciseness of your pendulum tunings benefiting yourself and others.

Life Energies

PHYSICAL

The word physical has the word physic as its root. Physics is the study of the structure of matter, and its forces, frequencies and fields. Our physical-self, our physiological organism - our body is dynamic. It is not a blob of lifeless matter. Rather, as the root word physics indicates, it is a vibrating structure of inter-working energy levels.

The body cells are energy systems not prison cells. Our cells are composed of molecules, and molecules are built up of atoms. Atoms are not solid stuff either. Instead, atoms are super-microscopic solar systems held together by positive and negative charges. As our solar system is mostly the fullness of space so too are the little realms of atoms.

Unfortunately, many, if not most of us, on this planet unconsciously cling to a deeply ingrained false-to-fact concept of the physical realm. We, without knowing it, believe the body to be a solid brick object, a mere thing.

The results of this subconscious mind-set affects the way we treat ourselves and others. We tend to approach the body as a dead thing instead of as a dynamic energy system operating according to natural order laws - normal temperatures and pressures, nutritional requirements, air and water quality, etc.

When I use the word "physical" in this book and in the context of the eight-spoked wheel of whole living, I mean it in the context of a dynamic, organic energy system.

Tune-in to your physical-self or the physical self of others with the pendulum. Draw out the eight-spoked wheel on a piece of paper. Lay it on a table in front of you. Hold the pendulum over the physical arc. Ask, is so and so's physical life energy channel balanced at this time?

If yes, you can check the degree of balance; if not the degree of imbalance. Proceed as follows. Write down a vertical column of numbers descending from 10 to 0.

If you received a yes answer begin with 10. Ask, is so and so's physical life energy a 10 at this time? Continue down the scale until you receive a yes rotation. With a no reading begin at 0 and work your way up until you get a yes response.

A no reading from 0 - 6 indicates a need for an individual to take note, see specifically what seems to be the matter and proceed to take constructive steps to eliminate the cause of imbalance. Chapter 9, Health and Healing Pendulum, will go into greater detail. Diet, exercise, fresh air, rest and so on can be checked to see where the possible sources of imbalance lie.

EMOTIONAL

What is an emotion? An emotion is a life energy, a vibrational force experienced as an automatic "inner motion". Emotion is usually a reactive force. We do not consciously choose to be emotional. An emotion happens. It springs suddenly from the psychological field like a jack out of its box.

Emotional energy surges, rises and falls, lifts and inspires, depresses and destroys. Suppressed and repressed emotions harm, in the long run, just as much as a blow to the head with a baseball bat. Excessive and compulsive emotions drain the life force, create havoc in our relationships and, block us from accomplishing our hearts desire.

Becoming conscious of your emotional life energies presents a great opportunity. The tide of emotion can be harnessed and directed. The power it generates may be the drive behind an invention, a painting, a business, a family and so on.

To check anyone's emotional balance follow the same steps followed in checking the physical life energy. All eight life energy channels can be checked using those steps. (fill in the blank).

1. Hold the pendulum over the _____ arc of the eight-spoked wheel diagram.

2. Ask, is so and so's _____ life energy balanced at this time?

3. A yes answer, proceed to check the degree of balance using a 0 - 10 scale. Start with 10. Ask, is so and so's _____ life energy at 10 at this time? Continue down the scale until you receive a yes reply.

4. A no answer, begin at 0 and work your way up until you get a yes response.

MENTAL

The mental-field of life energy is characterized by the activity of thought. What is a thought? Thought is a vibration, frequency, force recorded or registered in the mental-field.

There are many different levels of thought including: automatic, subjective, correlative, creative, rational, inspirational and ideational. An entire book could be devoted to defining, explaining and citing specific examples of each.

The well-rounded pendulumist must become conscious of the mental-field of activity. Try the following. Lay the book aside for a few moments. Close your eyes. Observe your mental-field. What's happening? Is your mental-field quiet, still, peaceful? Is it like a deep, calm crystal clear mountain lake without a ripple? Or, is it a fierce ocean with waves rising and falling crashing uncontrollably on the shores of your brain?

An expert pendulumist steadies the mental life energies, especially during readings. Thought-waves and thought forms are under his or her command. A clear mental-field is mandatory for clear questions and answers.

To check anyone's mental balance, again follow the steps outlined.

CREATIVE

Creative life energy has a soothing, time slowing, catharsis affect on the psyche, body, nervous system. Color, music, invention, form, imagination, movement - these are just some of the dynamics of creativity.

Tapping your creative energies and channeling them constructively adds another dimension to living. Over the years, I have tuned-in to thousands of individuals using the eight-spoked wheel of whole living as a map. The creative arc has consistently been one of the most neglected life areas.

Often, when I get a reading of 5 or below, the person reacts by saying, "I'm not creative; I can't do anything well." There seems to be a blockage in the American psyche regarding the tapping and channeling of creative energy.

The tendency is to automatically believe that born genius talent is required to be creative. Nothing could be further from the truth. To sing, you do not have to have a voice like Barbra Streisand. Sing; stop being identified with the ideal of singing and what others think about your singing.

Creativity is the playfulness of the soul. Avoiding it, denying it, repressing it, as a result, the creative life energy will not flow with balance. It then has a tendency to invert and flow destructively. Many so called "negative" people are highly gifted and talented. Unfortunately, their creative juices have not found a constructive outlet.

RELATIONSHIPS

Relating life energy connects us. Many are not conscious of its flow. What do you feel when you meet a new person? What do you feel when you meet someone close to you? Do you feel the flow, the relating life energy?

The well-rounded pendulumist who anticipates eventually giving readings for friends and clients would benefit immensely from becoming more conscious of relating energy. How can that be done? Whoever you meet each day practice conscious sensitivity, reception of vibrations from others.

What do you feel between you and another? Is there a meeting of the minds, easy communication and friendly smiles? Or is there disagreement, misunderstanding and antagonism? Between these two extremes there are many degrees. Learning conscious sensitivity to the nuances of relating energy will give you an excellent tool for navigating through the world of people.

When you receive an answer indicating someone's relating energies are out of balance, it may be the person is going through a divorce or an ongoing conflict with someone. Or, it might point to a reclusive tendency. Perhaps they have experienced too much hurt. Now they need to lick their wounds. Still another reason might be a retreat from others after a demanding cycle of relating energy activity.

Whatever the reason, restoring balance to the relationship area of life will increase a person's vitality, inner harmony and joy of sharing. A long term imbalance in this area may lead to dangerous sociopathic problems. Most criminal, violent and reclusive people have lost their relating energy balance. They require long term functional self-help in order to bring back a natural flow with others.

FINANCIAL

An endless string of semantic reactions are evoked when this word is used. Next to religion and politics, finances is one of the most emotionally charged topics.

Still, without any shadow of a doubt, our competitive, profit-oriented, banking system society demands that we earn, manage and, if possible, invest our money.

It is not uncommon when checking this life energy arc to find excessive imbalances. The business-person who devotes 12 and 15 hour days, year in and year out, is headed for trouble, problems, pain and suffering.

Too much life energy channeled into one life area takes away, literally robs life energy from flowing into the other seven life channels. Financial tycoons often marry and divorce several times, neglect their nutritional and exercise needs and tend to remain emotionally fixated at a certain level.

Oddly enough, at the other end of the spectrum, you find the so called poor people neglecting a well-rounded lifestyle. The constant demands for money, for food, rent and clothing creates similar imbalances as the rich.

Both extremes need to take a more level-headed look at their attitudes toward the financial life energy. The money warlord needs to get off the competitive, survival of the fittest frequency and be more creative with their riches, then, take conscious steps toward living a more well-rounded lifestyle. Those with the "lack mentality" must broaden their horizons, realize that the financial pinch they're in is the result of an "inner fear" of never having enough. The "inner fear" insecurity attracts financial instability.

To more thoroughly clarify the point I'm trying to make, I recommend reading Wallace D. Wattles classic, **Financial Success Through the Power of Creative Thought**. Written around the turn of the 20th century, there are several reprints published. I have written an abridged version called **Scientific Financial Success** which shortens and updates the content. (Write to Life Energy Sciences for ordering information. See address in the back of this book.)

From **Scientific Financial Success**:

"There is a science of financial success. If you apply this science you will, without doubt, become financially stable and balanced. By becoming financially successful you will make the most of yourself. Thus, you can be of greater service to god and humanity."

REGENERATIVE

Regenerative life energy transmutes old ways into new. When someone becomes aware of a trait, attitude, habit or behavior which they want to eliminate it takes regenerative life energy to change it.

Regeneration is actually an ongoing process. In ancient Egyptian religion the renewal, rebirth process was symbolized by the actions of the scarab beetle. It would roll itself up in a ball of dung and 30 days later emerge reborn.

Now, if you, a friend or client is not consciously channeling regenerative life energy, chances are the reading will be negative. You will pick up a positive reading from those who are consciously going through self-change, self-improvement, self-help.

It seems when the regenerative energies are not consciously directed the tendency is for regeneration to invert and flow compulsively into degeneration. By degeneration, I mean life energy is funneled into self-destructive behavior.

On the physical level excesses may include smoking, drinking, drugs and over-eating. On the emotional level it might be anger, impatience, resentment, hostility and fear. On the mental level it might manifest as excessive reading and studying, rigid adherence to certain dogmas or belief systems and just plain thinking too much.

On the creative arc of experience life energy may degenerate into compulsive creative work leading to the "poor, struggling artist" syndrome. Nothing else matters. Art for art's sake. Creativity blinds them. Their ego inflates with self-centered helium manufactured by their own fantasies.

Inverted relating life energies I previously mentioned. Criminal, antisocial and reclusive tendencies surface. And the lack of regenerative force in the financial life, as you just read, leads to poverty or compulsive wealth.

Most of us do not hear the word regeneration very often. Most of us do not know when, how or where to tap it and consciously channel it. Still, it's about time this neglected life energy be known. God knows we need it in our daily lives in order to grow, evolve and change. Stagnation is death. Without conscious regeneration there's unconscious degeneration.

SPIRITUAL

The other day a very perceptive person interested in the pendulum stopped by my office. He was curious how he might use the pendulum to change his life. With his permission I proceeded to dowse (tune-in to) his structure using the eight-spoked wheel of whole living.

He was relatively balanced through the first seven life arcs. When I asked, "is so and so's spiritual life energy balanced at this time?" I noticed him shift in his chair, turn his head down, roll his eyes back slightly and fidget with his fingers.

My new friend experienced a semantic reaction. In fact, it was so strong that I could not do the reading right away. I paused. I looked at him. I attempted to explain, the best I could in words, what I meant by the word "spiritual". I proceeded.

"To me the word 'spiritual' refers to non-verbal frequencies that can be directly experienced. Spiritual frequencies, vibrations and wavelengths oscillate at a higher rate than say, mental or emotional life energies."

I went on to say that, "to me spiritual does not mean dogma, fixed beliefs, blind faith or the reliance on the revelatory experience of someone else.

"No one else can eat and digest your food for you. Why should someone else have spiritual experiences for you? The direct experiencing of spiritual frequencies brings peace, perception, strength, knowledge, understanding, wisdom, will and love." "Knowing that," I said "how can anyone worship blindly?"

His semantic reaction passed. I was able to tune-in to his spiritual frequencies.

SUMMARY

1. To be conscious is to be acutely aware. When you are conscious, people, places and things are more immediate, more alive, more dynamic.

2. Becoming conscious is a journey into now, an adventure into the cosmic sea.

3. Practice the consciousness raising exercise. It will build up your awareness muscle. It will become a priceless tool for improved living.

4. The more conscious the pendulumist the more likely he or she will be able to pick up, detect, receive, feel, etc., the ultra-subtle frequencies that are tuned-in.

5. The eight-spoked wheel of whole living symbolizes the many interrelated areas of life you and I experience.

6. Becoming and being a dynamic well-rounded pendulumist requires, demands, taking a good look at yourself. Using the eight-spoked wheel diagram as a mirror, take a look.

7. Most all of us behave based on (1) reflection and (2) reaction. We tend to be activated automatically by reflection and/or reaction.

8. Your physical-self, your physiological organism - your body is dynamic. It is not a blob of lifeless matter. Rather, as the root word physics indicates, it is a vibrant structure of inter-working energy levels.

9. Unfortunately, many, if not most of us, on this planet unconsciously cling to a deeply ingrained false-to-fact concept of the physical realm. We, without knowing it, believe the body to be a solid brick object, a mere thing.

10. The results of this subconscious mind-set affects the way we treat ourselves and others. We tend to approach the body as a dead thing instead of as a dynamic energy system operating according to natural order laws - normal temperatures and pressures, nutritional requirements, air and water quality, etc.

11. An emotion is a life energy, a vibrational force experienced as an automatic "inner motion". Emotion is usually a reactive force. We do not consciously choose to be emotional. An emotion happens. It springs suddenly from the psychological-field like a jack out of its box.

12. Becoming conscious of your emotional life energies presents a great opportunity. The tide of emotion can be harnessed and directed. The power it generates may be the drive behind an invention, a painting, a business, a family and so on.

13. The mental-field of life energy is characterized by the activity of thought. What is a thought? Thought is a vibration, frequency, force recorded or registered in the mental-field.

14. An expert pendulumist steadies the mental life energies, especially during readings. Thought waves and thought forms are under his or her command. A clear mental-field is mandatory for clear questions and answers.

15. Creative life energy has a soothing, time-slowing affect on the psyche, body, nervous system.

16. Creativity is the playfulness of the soul. Avoiding it, denying it, repressing it - the creative life energy will not flow with balance. It then has the tendency to invert and flow destructively.

17. Relating life energy connects us. Learning conscious sensitivity to the nuances of relating energy will give you an excellent tool for negotiating through the world of people.

18. Our competitive, profit-oriented, banking system society demands that we earn, manage and, if possible, invest our money.

19. Both extremes, rich and poor, need to take a more level-headed look at their attitudes toward the financial life energy.

20. Regenerative life energy transmutes old ways into new. When someone becomes aware of a trait, attitude, habit, or behavior which they want to eliminate it takes regenerative life energy to change it.

21. It's about time this neglected life energy be known. God knows we need it in our daily lives in order to grow, evolve and change. Without conscious regeneration there's unconscious degeneration.

22. Spiritual frequencies, vibrations and wavelengths oscillate at a higher rate than say mental or emotional life energies.

23. Spiritual does not mean dogma, fixed beliefs, blind faith or the reliance on the revelatory experience of someone else.

24. The direct experiencing of spiritual frequencies brings peace, perception, strength, knowledge, understanding, wisdom, will and love.

CHAPTER 7: LOVE PENDULUM

Relationship Levels

A friend called up one day and asked me if I could use the pendulum to help him in a relationship. He had just been through a nasty divorce. The animosity, resentment and anger between him and his ex-wife understandably made him reluctant to begin a new relationship. He did not want to make another mistake.

He called me to ask about a woman whom he had just met. He was attracted to her. They talked a few times. She seemed attracted to him. Still, the thought of getting mixed up in another relationship conflict was unbearable.

I could feel his distress, concern and worry so I told him to come over and we would run a compatibility check between him and the woman he just met.

Fred arrived. We sat down at the kitchen table. On a blank piece of paper I drew two columns of five circles side by side. Above each column of circles I drew a horizontal line. In-between the two horizontal lines I drew a third line. On that line I wrote down the date (remember "*when indexing*"?).

Above the right hand column of circles I wrote Fred's name. I asked him the woman's name. I wrote that above the left hand column of circles. Next, in-between adjacent circles, I wrote, from top to bottom, the words spiritual, mental, energy, emotional, physical (See Figure 6 on the next page).

Now we were ready to ask the questions. At this time are Sarah and Fred "physically" compatible? I explained what I meant by "physically", the body vibrations mesh to some degree or clash to some degree.

The answer was yes. I then asked one after the other "at this time, using a 0 - 10 scale, is the physical compatibility between Sarah and Fred 6, 7, 8, 9, 10? I started at six because I know there was some degree of physical harmony.

I got a positive swing on 7. I wrote that down in the space between the two circles with the word "physical".

We went on to the "emotional" level. I asked, "at this time are Sarah and Fred "emotionally" compatible?" I explained by "emotional" I meant likes, dislikes, beliefs, background, etc. This time the pendulum did not rotate readi-

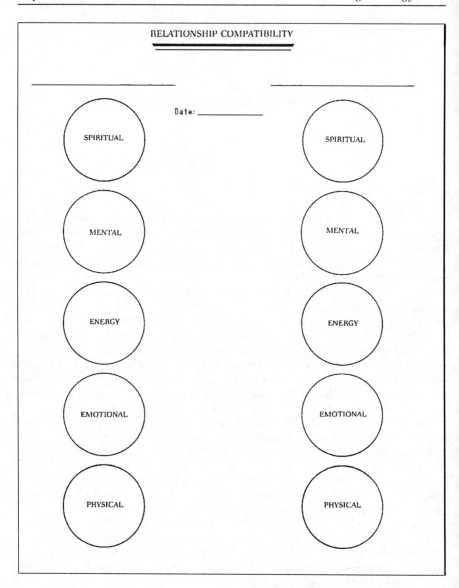

Figure 6: Relationship Compatibility.

ly. Finally, after 30 seconds or so, the pendulum started to swing, almost reluctantly, in a clockwise direction, a yes.

I proceeded to check the 0 - 10 scale as before. This time, though, I began with the number 5, I checked no further; the pendulum gave an immediate "yes" response. I wrote the number 5 in the space between the two "emotional" circles.

On to the "energy" level. By "energy" I told him I meant "when the two of you are together you feel energized, drained or somewhere in-between. The energy compatibility answer: Yes/9.

Continuing the relationship compatibility check with the "mental" level, I asked again and I gave my referent for the word "mental". Mental compatibility has to do with mind-sets, communication, word-systems, concepts and ideas.

A Polish communist and a Polish catholic may never be mentally compatible. Life views can be so opposite that under the present circumstances there's little possibility of clear communications.

The mental compatibility answer was Yes/8. I wrote an eight in the space between the "mental" level circles.

Moving on to the "spiritual" level I proceeded in the same way as before. I asked the question, "at this time, are Sarah and Fred "spiritually" compatible?" I clarified the pivotal word as before.

The spiritual level is a high frequency band of consciousness. It is not religious dogma. It is conscious experiencing of frequencies, forces and fields in many dimensions, including our three dimensions. Two individuals may have very similar or very different ways of experiencing spiritual realities.

The spiritual compatibility answer was Yes/9. I wrote a nine in the space between the "spiritual" circles.

Relationship Compatibility Rating

"That's interesting, but what does it mean?" probed Fred in a perplexed tone.

"Alright, let's get into that," I replied.

"First of all, look at the overview; take a whole picture of the relationship compatibility diagram. What do you see?"

"Mostly the answers were yes and the numbers above 5. I guess it looks fairly good," Fred said with a touch of understandable scepticism.

I continued the overview interpretation. "The way things look right now I'd have to rate this relationship as excellent. Here's how I arrived at that conclusion. If all five relationship spheres received a 10 reading the maximum total for all levels would be 5 x 10 = 50. Multiply that times two and you get 100% compatibility.

"Here's how I rate relationships." I wrote out the following:

Relationship Rating:

90 to 100	=	Superior
75 to 89	=	Excellent
50 to 74	=	Good
49 & Below	=	Poor

"I see," Fred exclaimed eagerly, "you added up the numbers between Sarah and I. Okay, nine plus eight plus....we total 38. Times two; we have a 76% which is excellent."

"You got it Fred; don't get too excited though. Remember "*when indexing*"; that's the way it looks today. A relationship compatibility check should be run between you and Sarah several times over a few weeks. And, even more importantly, take note of your experiences with Sarah. How do you feel when you're with her? Are you energized when you're with her?"

"Your advice is well taken. I see what you mean. The relationship compatibility check is not the relationship."

"Right, it's simply a way of becoming more aware of what's happening between people.

"Also, a 76% reading is on the border between good and excellent. So the way it looks now there might be a few conflicts here and there to keep things interesting.

"Besides, all relationships are dynamic, not static. We live in an energy universe. Relationships release and generate energy.

"At any given moment an overall superior relationship could temporarily become a poor relationship if a spontaneous conflict arises. On the other hand, a generally poor relationship could, in moments, be an excellent or even, occasionally, a superior relationship."

Compatibility Interpretation

Fred wanted to know more. "Now that I have an idea Sarah and I will probably get along, what else can you tell me?"

"We see the overview, a 76% rating. Next, we look at the different levels and interpret the numerical readings."

"The emotional level looks like trouble," Fred declared emphatically. "I'm not sure how much more I can take right now."

"Hold on Fred," I interjected trying to steady him a bit. Look at the facts. What's Sarah's background?"

"She comes from a big city and a big family..."

"See; that one difference alone could be the major reason for the five. Fred, based on the many readings I have done, I'd say Sarah and you have a pretty good chance of developing a lasting relationship. You're compatible now in 4 out of 5 spheres. You're 8 and 9's in the top three levels.

"Often I've done readings with high compatibility on the physical and emotional levels and low compatibility on the spiritual, mental and energy levels. Those kinds of relationships seem to never last. They're here today and gone tomorrow. Strong physical attractions and exciting emotions feel real good but fade away in a month to six months."

"So you're saying with Sarah and I, it's not just a flash in the pan."

"Right. There's a physical attraction but with the seven she's probably not your ideal nor are you hers."

"You're exactly right," replied Fred with some surprise.

"Now with the nine energy reading you more than likely feel tremendously energized and rejuvenated after being together."

Fred nodded, yes.

"With the 8 mental and 9 spiritual you probably talk about deeper, more meaningful topics, and you tend to see eye to eye on those topics.

"You're right again," Fred acknowledged.

"So, in summary, I'd say go ahead despite your natural feelings of hesitation. Take it slow. It will take time for the different likes and dislikes and personal backgrounds on the emotional level to come to light and be accepted and understood. Share your inner goals, ideals and dreams and consider your relationship a good friendship for now. Let it unfold. You do not have to rush. Go your own pace."

Fred thanked me for the reading. I told him to call anytime to check it again. I repeated the importance of tuning to the relationship at different times, "*when indexing*".

Fred and Sarah became friends. A year later, they began living together. Three years after that they got married. Now, on their third wedding anniversary, they are having their first child.

Love

During my first years with the pendulum I came across a situation that eventually taught me a good lesson. I was in a stage where my readings were 75 - 80% accurate and others recognized my skill.

Through a friend of mine at work I met her friend, Elaine. Elaine worked for a major airline as a flight attendant and supervisor. Being in her early twenties, on her time off, she would look for Mr. Right.

That's where I came in. Elaine was fascinated by the pendulum, overly so, as I eventually realized. She instantly saw how she could ask questions about the men she met. The question was, "does so and so love me?"

As first I didn't mind asking this question. But as the days and weeks went by and Elaine asked me over and over about the same guy and then someone new, and then another and another. I realized I had to clarify the word "love".

Every time she had me do a pendulum reading and the word "love" was in the question something just did not seem right. I could not put my finger on it. Finally, after two months, it dawned on me, the "love" Elaine was asking about was not the "love" I thought when tuning-in.

Also it hit me that if a person has to ask if someone "loves" them chances are that person doesn't love them or they cannot feel the "love" coming from that person. Regardless, the love connection is not experienced.

Finally, one night when Elaine called for her reading and she asked "does so and so love me?" I responded by asking, "what do you mean by the word "love", Elaine? If I knew, I know my accuracy will improve."

Elaine remained silent for a few seconds. Her tongue was tied. Finally, she undid the knot. It's "good feelings" and "kindness", she answered.

"In that case," I responded, "how do you feel when you're around so and so?"

"He's really good looking and nice."

"How do you feel though?" I repeated.

"I don't know. A little uptight I guess."

That reply hit me like a ton of bricks. Elaine had never truly experienced a loving relationship with a man. What she was really asking was "what is love and how do I experience it? Not "does so and so love me?"

From that day forward I began using the relationship compatibility check, a more precise and specific way of seeing the "love" or potential love between people.

Trying to verbalize the non-verbal experience of love is virtually impossible. Elaine's silence was perhaps the closest answer. The experience "love" is forever on the unspeakable level.

To say what it is, is probably best said, if we must, by what it is not. It is not possessiveness; it is not selfishness. It is not sex; it is not domination; it is not being dominated. It is not using another; it is not manipulating, etc.

Marriage

When the honeymoon is over and a couple live together for awhile the romance reality is modified or replaced by the "relationship reality". By relationship reality I mean each begins to develop through experience with each other a totally different picture and, more importantly, perception of the other.

The bubble bursts. You see the ugly side. You work more, play less. There are responsibilities to take care of.

If the love bond is strong the relationship reality will continue; you have a marriage.

On the other hand, if the romance reality was the marriage foundation then the relationship reality is too shocking. The marriage ends in divorce; the love bond is weak.

The pendulum can contribute much to a marriage. When tensions, conflicts, misunderstandings and pressing questions arise in the marriage a pendulum reading can quickly shine a light on the difficulty.

Awareness is magic. Awareness is laser light penetrating the muck of ignorance, unconsciousness and the pressure points of the past.

Awareness dissipates and dissolves the clouds of doom and gloom. Awareness lights the dark night of the soul with the suns of clarity.

Tuning-in to the marriage relationship from time to time will bring a sensitivity and an understanding of the other's feelings, thoughts and views.

So often we cannot express what we are feeling. One of the love partners may be going through difficult emotional times. You ask then, "what's the matter?" They may respond, "I don't know" or "nothing".

With the pendulum you can find out what's going on immediately. Check it out. Ask the pendulum a series of specific questions. The yes answers along with the 0 - 10 scale readings can pinpoint the problem.

You may find out that the strain on the marriage has nothing much to do with your relationship; it may be some outside influence. Or, indeed, there may be some distressing problem in the marriage. Better to know and deal with it than let it eat away your love.

Here is a list of questions which may assist you in tracking down the relationship wrecker.

"Is there something specific that I do?; I say?; I think?; I feel?; I believe?, which turns off so and so?"

If you receive a yes answer to any of these, get more specific. For example, a yes on "I do" can be narrowed down to particular actions like smoking, drinking too much, watching a lot of television, forgetting to lock the car...etc., etc. You have to ask the questions based on your personal history together.

A no answer to the above series of questions may indicate the problem lies within the other person - something they do, say, think, feel or believe - or outside the relationship reality, at work, in the community, with friends, etc. Once you've pinpointed the source, defined the problem or problems, then you can create a plan together which will maintain a high level of harmony in the marriage. Or, the hard truth may be that your marriage is reaching an end. The cycle is closing. You met, loved, married, shared life together, learned your lessons and now its time to move on.

Friendship

A common complaint today is: "It's hard to make friends." It seems a lot of friendships begin strong but fizzle out quickly. We move more. We are more self-centered. We are more impersonal. Times have changed. The kind of friendships people were used to in the past have, for the most part vanished.

Today friendships often have little to do with how long you have known someone or what you have gone through together, although that is still a valid way of establishing a friendship. As we make the transition into a new age race psyche, friendships will occur "spontaneously", anytime and anywhere.

The law of sympathetic vibration may be explained as follows: when at least two persons, places or things (or combinations) resonate/vibrate at the same frequency they are in sympathetic vibration. In other words, there's a powerful attraction - energy exchange.

I was talking to a friend yesterday who had just met someone who he "instantly" made friends with. "It was as if we had known each other for years," he commented. Having gone through some so called friendship where he was left holding the bag, he naturally, was concerned about making the same mistake again.

I did a relationship compatibility check as presented in the first two sections of this chapter. These were the readings at that time: physical 9, emotional 8, energy 10, mental 8, spiritual 8. The relationship compatibility rating is determined by adding up the 5 numbers, (43) and multiplying by two, 86%. Taking a glance at the relationship rating chart on page 57, 86% is an excellent rating, toward the upper end of the range, close to superior.

"No wonder you felt like instant friends," I explained. Many new age friendships will form "quickly", "spontaneously", "instantly". The reason I place quotation marks around these words is because they are, in a way, prejudiced terms. From the belief system that "friendships take time" it may seem fast. The law of sympathetic vibration supercedes time cycles. As one new age teacher/writer put it "your being attracts your life".

Begin to take careful note of the kinds of people you spend a lot of time with. There's an old saying that birds of feather flock together. In other words, those people you call friends will in some way, often in many ways, reflect your own tendencies, attitudes, habits, likes and dislikes, etc.

The Buddha once gave some advice along these lines.

If you do not have a friend
sober, pure and wise
walk alone -- like a king who
has renounced a conquered
kingdom,
or an elephant roaming free

in the forest.
Better aloneness than the
friendship of a fool
Walk alone like an elephant
roaming free in the forest
be undemanding. Stay away
from unconsciousness.
Choose friends virtuous and excellent
shun the low-minded and
ill-doing.

From the **Dhammapada**

SUMMARY

1. All relationships are dynamic, not static. We live in an energy universe. Relationships release and generate energy.

2. At any given moment an overall superior relationship could temporarily become a poor relationship if a generally poor relationship could, in moments, be an excellent or even occasionally a superior relationship.

3. The relationship rating is simply a way of becoming more aware of what's happening between people.

4. Often I've done readings with high compatibility on the physical and emotional levels and low compatibility on the spiritual, mental and energy levels. Those kind of relationships seem to never last. They're here today and gone tomorrow. Strong physical attractions and exciting emotions feel real good but fade away in a month to six months.

5. Trying to verbalize the non-verbal experience of "love" is virtually impossible. The experience "love" is forever on the unspeakable level.

6. To say what love is, is probably best said, if we must, by what it is not. It is not possessiveness. It is not selfishness; it is not sex. It is not dominating; it is not being dominated; it is not using another; it is not manipulation, etc.

7. When the honeymoon is over and a couple live together for awhile the romance reality is modified or replaced by the "relationship reality".

8. The bubble bursts. You see the ugly side. You work more, play less. There are responsibilities to take care of. If the love bond is strong the relationship reality will continue; you have a marriage.

9. The pendulum can contribute much to a marriage. When tensions, conflicts, misunderstandings and pressing questions arise in the marriage, the pendulum can quickly shine light on the difficulty.

10. Awareness is magic. Awareness is laser light penetrating the muck of ignorance, unconsciousness and the pressure points of the past. Awareness dissipates and dissolves the clouds of doom and gloom. Awareness lights the dark night of the soul with the suns of clarity.

11. Tuning-in to the marriage relationship from time to time will bring a sensitivity and an understanding of the other's feelings, thoughts and views.

12. As we make the transition into a new age race psyche friendships will occur "spontaneously", anytime, anywhere.

13. The law of sympathetic vibration may be explained as follows: when at least two persons, places or things (or combinations) resonate/vibrate at the same frequency they are in sympathetic vibration. In other words, there's a powerful attraction - energy exchange.

14. Many new age friendships will form quickly, spontaneously, instantly. The law of sympathetic vibration supercedes time cycles. As one new age teacher/writer put it "your being attracts your life".

CHAPTER 8: CAREER/BUSINESS/FINANCE

Choosing a Career

How can you choose a career, the type of work that's right for you? Once again the pendulum is a useful tool.

Nothing is more tragic than a person choosing a career or vocation that does not suit them. The mental, emotional and relationship strain can, and usually does, make everyday life difficult, to say the least.

If a person comes to you with a career question, hopefully they have some general idea where their talent and skills lie. Be that the case, then you can ask the appropriate questions.

Early in 1984 a woman asked me to help her determine where she should focus her career/work energies. She was very talented; several skills had to be checked.

First we wrote down all the areas which she was interested in pursuing. They were: writing, mail order numerology charts, psychic readings and teaching.

I went down the line asking the following question on a 0 - 10 scale how wise would it be for Terry to focus her work energies on (1) writing - 8, (2) mail order numerology - 7, (3) psychic readings - 8 and (4) teaching - 10.

She couldn't wait to get started. I told her to try it out for a month and see if it tested out against the life-facts.

She immediately organized self-help classes. Within a month things were rolling. The first class was full, so she set up a second. The response amazed her.

Writing and psychic readings received eights. She pursued those career goals also. Both of them generated additional income but were not as strong as the teaching.

Nine months after the initial meeting Terry has quite a local following studying new age topics. Her students are thankful for the regular classes.

In Terry's case, the pendulum helped her clarify what she already knew. She just needed to set priorities and then act decisively on those priorities. Thank goodness she had the common sense to act on the pendulum reading.

Before I continue I would like to clear up what is called in general semantics, a high order abstraction. In Terry's question I used the word "wise". By "wise" I meant, relative to Terry's life path, would it be in her best interests in terms of her overall development.

It is not wise to touch a hot stove. Inevitably you burn your hand - pain and suffering result. It is wise for Terry to teach new age topics. For her not to teach would more than likely lead to frustration.

Now, when someone comes to you who has little if any idea what kind of work they should be doing, it can be a bit more difficult to determine specific career goals.

First, you might ask them what they are interested in or, if they woke up tomorrow doing what they really wanted, what would it be?

Check those areas first. Nines and tens indicate strong career tendencies. Still, if they have not put too much energy into those areas much time may have to pass before they can stabilize that life work.

The pendulum can speed up the process some by outlining efficient steps. For example, you might ask "is it wise for so and so to go back to school to learn such and such a vocation?" If yes, you can determine which school would be best for them.

If schooling is not the best means to starting a career perhaps work experience would be better. Ask and see.

In the meantime, while training for a new career, if it's not on the job training, then you can check temporary job opportunities to see which would generate income plus give them necessary work experiences.

Another way to help determine a compatible career for someone is to get a job list from the library or make your own from the classified section of your local newspaper. Go down the list. It may take some time but it is well worth it if a person can find their true calling.

The individual you are doing the reading for may be pleasantly surprised to discover a career area which they have never considered yet suits them perfectly.

The more of us who find our life work the more harmonious we feel. As a result, the workplace and our society become more harmonious as well.

Starting a Business

Besides choosing a career with the pendulum you can choose a business. The steps are the same. However, I would suggest asking one pertinent question before proceeding. I'll tell you what it is in a second.

In 1980 a student came to me with a pressing question. It seems he had a powerful urge to start his own haircutting shop. At the same time he had an over-powering fear of failure. He loved the image of himself as his own boss. He liked the freedom, the money and the respect.

Unfortunately, several years before he owned a corner grocery store which burned to the ground. The trauma of the fire had shaken him deeply. Although he wanted to start another business, he knew he could not stand another major disaster.

So I proceeded to ask the following question, a question that should be asked first before starting a business. "Is it wise for Frank to start a business at this time and specifically a haircutting business?" I held my arm steady. The pendulum began to rotate - yes.

I followed that question with "on a 0 - 10 scale how wise is it for Frank to start a haircutting business?" I worked my way up the scale from 5 until the pendulum responded positively at 9. It looked like a go.

Frank was pleased. Still, he felt afraid and nervous. I suggested he not worry. Take it one baby step at a time. I told him he did not have to make a move until **he** was sure it made sense.

I told him to go ahead and start making the plans; make some decisions about the size of the shop, the location, the employees, the name and the amount of monthly overhead. Then I told him to call me, set an appointment and we would check out his decisions with the pendulum.

A month passed. Frank gave me a call. We got together.

He had picked out three tentative locations for the shop. He gave me the exact addresses. I asked: "On a 0 - 10 scale how wise is it for Frank to start and establish a haircutting business at 2473 Stevens Avenue?" I repeated the question for the other two locations. The first address received a 5, the second a 2 and the third an 8.

The third address on Evans Avenue was by far the best but it was not a 9 or 10. Frank said the pendulum was probably picking up the fact that there were some contractual problems.

Apparently, the landlord wanted a 3 year lease at a higher monthly rate than Frank wished to pay. Frank wanted a 5 year lease at a lesser monthly rate with a 5 year option.

We moved on to the next question. Frank had a list of potential workers. I went down the list. "All things considered, quality of work, personality, compatibility, discipline etc., how wise is it to hire x, y, z, etc.?" We received a couple eights and a nine.

Anyway, we worked our way through a long list of specific questions, Often the pendulum agreed with Frank's plans giving him confirmation and confidence.

Today, several years later, he has a thriving business. He has the independence he wanted in order to pursue some of his avocations and hobbies.

An accurate pendulumist can be an invaluable business consultant as long as two critical points are carefully considered. One - what's your motivation and the motivation of the client? Two - do not let the pendulum's answers be the answer. Always insist that the head or heads of the business take the pendulum's answers into consideration in making **their** final decision.

The pendulum, even in the hands of a master pendulumist, is not always right for a variety of possible reasons. Remember - it is not omnicient; it is not the oracle.

Also consider motivation and intent. In other words, is your client motivated solely by greed and power or is it their desire to succeed so that the profits can be shared with loved ones and friends. Frank's intentions, for example, were honest. He needed the money to have the time to learn more about his consuming interest in health and healing.

The pendulum, it seems, has a way of being consistently inaccurate when the intentions are selfish. Apparently, selfishness is a low frequency which becomes an interference pattern blocking clear frequencies (answers).

Weekly Business Readings

During a three year stretch a business owner took weekly self-help classes which included business readings. Jim owned and operated a small construction company in an east coast metropolitan area. At the time he began with the classes and readings, business was slow.

It was a family construction business. Jim's father had started it some twenty-five years before. Jim and his brother now owned it. Mostly they did small remodeling, installation and repair jobs.

Neither one of us had any intention of using the pendulum to build a thriving, successful, medium-sized construction company. In truth, Jim was taking self-help lessons first and the pendulum was kind of an aside.

It was a great opportunity for me to explore uncharted pendulum regions. Also, Jim was excellent to work with. He had his own mind. He took the pendulum answers into consideration in making his business decisions. He did not rely solely on the pendulum responses.

The very first area of concern was his older brother. They were not getting along. We did a relationship compatibility check which verified Jim's experience.

He asked: "Is it wise for me to buy out my brother's half of the business?" The pendulum answered - yes. Then I checked the 0 - 10 scale. We got a nine.

Many more questions were asked and answered, "How much?", "when?", "how?", etc., were gone into.

In a couple months, Jim was sole owner of the small family construction company. He felt free. His big brother's dictatorial ways were behind him. He now could steer the company on a sane course.

We went into many business areas with the pendulum over the next three years. We regularly checked job applicants to see who would and would not do quality work. A high percentage of the time the pendulum was right. A

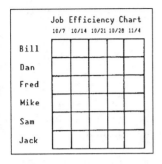

Figure 7: Job Efficiency Sheet

few times Jim hired people he liked rather than who he knew could do the job. The pendulum got low readings. It almost always did not work out.

We checked job efficiency and effort. Jim prepared a job efficiency sheet. See Figure 7 on this page. Each week, using the 0 - 10 scale, we measured job performance. This helped Jim tremendously. He became more conscious of who was and who was not doing their job. Again, the pendulum was highly accurate.

The awareness and conscious effort Jim applied to his small construction company began to pay off financially. The jobs were more plentiful. Jim decided to buy his own building.

The pendulum came in handy once again. He looked all over for a building. Each time he found one that might be right, I would check the pendulum. Without exception, every building that received a negative answer was either too much, not big enough, had poor location or it just did not work out.

Finally, though, we hit on a building. The pendulum received a 9 answer. The owner was willing to finance the building directly to Jim. Jim paid him the monthly payment which included interest. He did not have to go through a bank.

The building was less than a block from his old location so old customers could still find his new location easily. There was plenty of office space, shop space and a showroom. The investment and tax write offs did not hurt either.

Once a week Jim came up with the idea of checking the compatibility of employees in work situations. Most of Jim's workers had partners. The teams were paired as such: the more experienced leader and the less experienced helper.

The employee compatibility results were remarkable. We asked the following question of each team: "On a 0 - 10 scale how efficiently do (name) and (name) work together?"

According to the pendulum, many of the work teams were mismatched. Jim was reluctant to change teams around. Afterall, the business was thriving. I suggested he rematch a couple teams and test out the pendulum's accuracy. If it did not work out then he could always go back to the way he had it.

Not only did productivity go up, the workers seemed happier, more enthusiastic. Needless to say, all the construction teams were formed on the pendulum's tuning.

The growth of Jim's construction company was amazing over those three years of weekly readings. The pendulum was a major force in that growth as were Jim's experience and determination. The time was right as well. Everything, it seemed, wanted to come together. All the business needed was someone to fit the pieces together.

A Wall Street-Bear

Not all business and financial consultations are as successful, accurate and rewarding. A Wall Street analyst heard of my pendulum work and somehow got my number. He had done some work with the pendulum and could appreciate its potential use in the stock market.

From my very first conversation with Dick I felt uncomfortable about stock market readings. At first, I didn't know why. Still, I said yes to his request for pendulum instruction.

A few days later we met for our first class. Dick was a rather intense fellow in his early fifties. He was excited about the prospects of striking pay dirt in the market.

We reviewed the material in Chapter 4: "How to Use the Pendulum" for three weeks. In the meantime, Dick began formulating his questions. By the fourth week, the dam broke; a wall of questions poured out of him.

Here are some examples of just a few of his many questions. "How many points will such and such a stock go up in the next two weeks?" "What is the level of management skills at such and such a corporation?" "When will the Dow Average peak this year?" "Would it be wise for Dick to try stock X?" "Will gold go above the $1,000 mark this year?"

Anyway, it was a torrent of questions. Truthfully, it overwhelmed me, for a couple of reasons. One, I was not familiar with the language and lingo of Wall Street. Two, I felt Dick was in a hurry to strike it rich.

Still, I proceeded over the next several weeks to give lessons and to answer Dick's financial questions. Well, it only took those several weeks to see that my readings were not accurate, probably below 50%. Dick could have flipped a coin and received more accurate answers.

Needless to say, he stopped coming. I was not what he thought I was - an expert pendulumist who could dowse the answers to anything, anytime.

As I clearly discovered, the pendulum has its limitations. I spent several hours reviewing, analyzing, and digesting my experiences with Dick and his Wall Street world.

Several reasons for the inaccuracies came to mind. I was uncomfortable with the stock market world. The words confused me. The facts and figures made no sense to me. I realized that accuracy with the pendulum depends a great deal on the pendulumist having a rudimentary understanding of the area in question. The confusion and discomfort are static preventing clear reception.

Another reason for a low percentage was the intention of the questioner. As far as I was concerned, Dick's interest in the pendulum was primarily financial. He wanted to beat the system. To him the pendulum was a magic wand; wave it and riches would appear.

A third reason was the strong emphasis on future questions. Answering future questions is like trying to mold air into a visible shape with your hands. It cannot be done. The future is plastic. How we and others think, feel and desire today are the forces moving toward future events. If we and others change today how we think, feel and desire, then the future is altered as well.

These are the lessons I learned from the Wall Street Bear. Now, if I am uncomfortable with an area of knowledge, I tell the client I would rather not tune-in because of my lack of clarity. Or, if I take an interest, I may study the field enough to have a basic knowledge. Now, if a person has a greedy or selfish intention I try to avoid using the pendulum. Also, if a person wants a future question answered, I tell them the future is plastic; it is molded by today's thoughts, feelings and desires.

Streamlining Sales

If you are earning a living in sales, efficient use of your time and energy is a must. For commission only sales people wasting valuable time and energy can spell disaster. The pendulum can streamline the sales process; it cannot close the deal.

Most real estate agents depend on sales for income. Talent, discipline, knowledge, communication and a sense of timing contribute greatly to a real estate agent's level of success. To be acutely aware of what is happening between agent and client is critical, especially when it comes to buying a home.

Today home buyers are faced with high prices, the average home costs over $100,000. A real estate agent must be sensitive to the client's likes, dislikes, fears, misgivings and dreams.

The pendulum can be used effectively throughout the selling process as an awareness booster. For instance, let's say you have an open house. Twenty potential buyers come to the open house. Some talk to you, some say they are just looking and others come and go without saying a word.

You station a person at the front door to greet and welcome everyone. They ask the visitors to sign the guest book. To a real estate agent with a pendulum skill that list of names is invaluable.

At the end of the day, while your memories are fresh, rewrite all the names, addresses and phone numbers on 3 x 5 cards. If you talked to someone, note the content of the conversation. Write down any perception which you feel could be significant in the selling process. Be sure to date all cards.

Now for the pendulum; hold the pendulum over each 3 x 5 card and ask: "Is so and so ready to buy a home at the present time?" Follow up a yes answer with a 0 - 10 scale check. Note and date your answer on the 3 x 5 card, for example, yes - 9, 5/7/85.

It should not take long for you to verify the accuracy of your answers. Those potential buyers with 8, 9, or 10 should receive followup letters and phone calls. If they are seriously in a market for a home, one or two conversations will reveal that sincere desire.

As you become more and more accurate with the pendulum at this initial stage, you will not waste time with "talkers". Some people talk like they want to buy but they are not, for one reason or other, ready to purchase a home (or any other product or service).

Knowing who is ready, willing and able to buy a home and who is not means more efficient use of your time. You will devote more time to making the sale and less time to finding and developing prospective buyers.

There are numerous other questions that could be asked as the agent-buyer relationship develops. You can formulate specific questions regarding price range, neighborhoods and home design preferences.

Again, for more efficient use of time, you can go down the list of homes for sale and ask the following: on a 0 - 10 scale how compatible are Mr. & Mrs. Home Buyer with the home located at 2710 Bell Drive?"

Compatibility readings of 8, 9 and 10 indicate homes that Mr. & Mrs. Home Buyer should see first. Your clients will appreciate seeing homes they like. It will create more enthusiasm in the sales process.

Obviously, liking a home does not mean they are going to buy it. A multitude of other factors have to be considered like price, location, schools, shopping, number of bedrooms, etc. Still, you will have the buyers on a positive track.

Any sales person reading between the lines will recognize the pendulum's potential in other sales fields. Remember, it will probably take time to perfect your skill and accuracy. Your strong hopes, wishes and desires will influence the pendulum's answers.

Learning to be neutral, knowing when and when not to do readings and asking specific questions will go a long way toward giving you a high percentage of accuracy in the sales area.

Short and Long Term Priorities

If your work demands setting priorities, the pendulum can help you order your day, week, month, year and longer. While traveling to work in the morning, no doubt a host of daily activities pop in and out of your head. Usually, there are one or two tasks that demand your immediate attention. Still, it does not hurt to write a list of daily activities once you arrive on the job.

Place the list of activities in front of you on the desk. Before taking out your pendulum consider the reactions of co-workers to seeing you use a pendulum. Be discreet if you must. There is no need to get people uptight.

Now, take out your pendulum. Using the 0 - 10 scale once again, begin with the first task on the list. Starting at 10 ask, "is writing a letter to the President of Widget International a 10 priority today?" If you get a no answer continue to 9, 8, 7, etc.

Once you receive a priority rating, write that number beside the appropriate task. Continue down the list following the same steps each time. After completing the list, ask this final question: "Am I forgetting an important task that needs my attention today?" A yes answer means think; try to recall.

Now, rewrite your daily priority list; at the top put all your tens. If you like, you can even put the tens in order of importance by tuning-in with the pendulum. Proceed with the nines, eight, sevens, etc.

Those activities with low priority rating may not be taken care of that day. Simply carry them over to the next day. Their priority level may change as the demand for their completion increases.

Naturally, it is advisable to remain flexible and alert to sudden changes in priorities. A big order, an unexpected sale, an important client stops by, expect the unexpected and adapt accordingly.

The process by which you set your daily priorities can be repeated for the weekly, monthly, yearly and longer. Flexibly setting priorities can go a long way toward helping you achieve what it is you want to achieve.

A clear image or mental map of where you want to go, what you want to achieve and then a level of priority means clarity and a commitment of life energy to the goal.

Without clear mental maps and high priority levels, goals pass in and out of the mind like wisps of intangible smoke. Fantasy not reality becomes the order of the day.

Assigning an order of importance to New Year's resolutions can also be determined using the priority rating method. Three or four possible resolutions may be floating through your consciousness. If one resolution is all you want to tackle in a year, then you can find out which demands your immediate attention. You may want to ask the following question: "All things considered, which New Year's resolution would be the wisest for me, x? y? z?"

SUMMARY

1. Nothing is more tragic than a person choosing a career or vocation that does not suit them. The mental, emotional and relationship strain can, and usually does, make everyday life difficult.

2. The more of us who find our life work the more harmonious we feel. As a result, the work place and our society become more harmonious as well.

3. An accurate pendulumist can be an invaluable business consultant as long as two critical points are carefully considered. One - your motivation and the motivation of your client? Two - do not let the pendulum's answers be the answer.

4. Is your client motivated solely by greed and power, or is it their desire to succeed so that the profits can be shared with loved ones and friends.

5. The pendulum is not always right for a variety of possible reasons. Remember - it is not omnicient; it is not an oracle.

6. The growth of Jim's construction company was amazing over the three years of weekly pendulum readings. The pendulum was a major force in that growth as were Jim's experience and determination.

7. As I clearly discovered, the pendulum has its limitations. I spent several hours reviewing analyzing and digesting my experiences with Dick and his Wall Street world.

8. I realized that accuracy with the pendulum depends a great deal on the pendulumist having a rudimentary understanding of the area in question.

9. Answering future questions is like trying to mold air into a visible shape with your hands. It can not be done. The future is plastic. How we and others think, feel, and desire today are the forces moving toward future events.

10. The pendulum can streamline the sales process; it cannot close the deal.

11. The pendulum can be used effectively throughout the selling process as an awareness booster.

12. Learning to be neutral, knowing when and when not to do readings and asking specific questions will go a long way toward giving you a high percentage of accuracy in the sales area.

13. If your work demands setting priorities, the pendulum can help you order your day, week, month, year and longer.

14. Naturally, it is advisable to remain flexible and alert to sudden changes in priorities. A big order, an unexpected sale, an important client stops by, expect the unexpected and adapt accordingly.

15. Without clear mental maps and high priority levels goals pass in and out of the mind like wisps of intangible smoke. Fantasy not reality becomes the order of the day.

CHAPTER 9: HEALTH AND HEALING PENDULUM

Beyond High Tech Medicine

A few weeks ago a woman asked a pendulumist, "Is my baby healthy?" This woman had been asking him pendulum questions on and off for years. She felt comfortable with the pendulum. He felt comfortable answering her questions with the pendulum.

The pendulumist failed to pay attention to the question. He went ahead and checked the pendulum. He got a 6 on a 0 - 10 scale.

The mother instantly became upset. She almost burst into tears. A six indicated, at least to her, that her baby might be sick.

Based on what you have read, learned and practiced do you see where the pendulumist messed up? Look at the question, "Is your baby healthy?"

Right. This question is too vague and general. He did not give a referent for the word "healthy". Additionally, he should have specifically named the baby.

He should have asked the mother what she felt might be physically wrong with Sarah, for example, lungs, stomach, intestines, etc. Then again, the word "health" does not have to automatically refer to "physical" organs or body parts.

Anyway, he settled her down. He told her the six answer meant little if anything since the question itself was practically meaningless.

Gentleman's Quarterly published an article in their health section titled "Playing Doctor: Eight Ways to Detect Ailments Early." The eighth section was headed with the word Radiesthesia, the French word for pendulum use.

Joseph Polansky, who co-authored **Pendulum Power** with me, was quoted by GQ as saying, "You can diagnose yourself or a friend by making a list of organs and, concentrating on one organ at a time, asking if that organ is healthy."

"Of course," Polansky cautions, "it can take as much as a year to become proficient. You have to make sure you're emotionally neutral about the situation; otherwise, you'll subconsciously influence the swing."

Obviously, the pendulumist who asked the question, "on a 0 - 10 scale how wise is it for me to go around playing doctor?" would find it is unwise to diagnose indiscriminately. Traditional bio-chemical medical diagnosis should not be abandoned. Caution and care should be used. It's one thing to ask a question about your own health, a family member or a close friend and another to ask health question about total strangers, the general public.

I know of one prominent doctor who wrote the following in the foreward to his unpublished research:

"I make no claim of diagnosis or treatments of any diseases or conditions in medicine as the pendulum is a biofeedback reaction between the practitioner and the patient. This is a personal choice of the practitioner using his own level of awareness."

I was fortunate to come across a copy of this doctor's lifetime of non-traditional diagnosis and therapy research using the pendulum. All his patients must read, sign and date a treatment consent form. The last paragraph reads: "I have read, understand and accept the above information. This consent form will be placed in your chart for a permanent record."

You better believe that if a doctor knowledgeable in both medicine and the pendulum is cautious you and I ought to be extra-cautious.

That said, what do I mean by "Beyond High Tech Medicine?" Health care costs are rising at a rate faster than you and I can afford. One of the major reasons for the astronomical increases is high tech medicine. Complicated surgical procedures like bone marrow and heart transplants cost in the hundreds of thousands. Highly technical and expensive testing equipment like catscans, a kind of brain x-ray machine, increase medical bills dramatically.

John Naisbitt in his bestseller **Megatrends** repeatedly underscores the "High Tech, High Touch" trend. For instance, banking executives believed electronic banking would free up procedures and eliminate personnel. To the contrary, customers across the country preferred personal teller service to an electronic teller, "High Tech, High Touch."

The pendulum in health and healing is high touch in a high tech medical world. The pendulum is a kind of new age stethoscope. It is one tool every health care specialist may eventually carry in their pocket.

A catscan machine costs over a million, most pendulums under twenty dollars. The pendulum in the hands of an expert can tune-in to the brain in seconds and determine where there is a physiological disorder.

In the long run maintaining your health at an optimum level will ward off sickness and disease more than anything. Before we check the Health Maintenance Dial let's tackle the word "health".

What is health? Health is a dynamic condition of physical, emotional, mental and spiritual balance which brings regenerating vitality to the cells, the instincts, the intellect and the intuition.

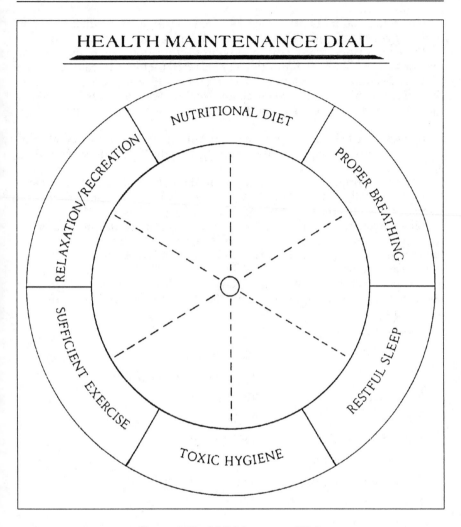

Figure 8: Health Maintenance Dial.

Look at the Health Maintenance Dial, Figure 8 above.

The Health Maintenance Dial focuses on the living physiological organism level. Taking care of your body affects your emotional, mental and spiritual equilibrium as well. All these levels are interconnected and interrelated.

Go to the Health Maintenance Dial. Use your finger as the dial, the index finger of your left hand if you're working the pendulum with your right.

Place your finger on the dial and point to "nutritional diet" and ask: "At this time is John Doe's diet nutritionally balanced for him?" Regardless of the answer, yes or no, follow up by checking the 0 - 10 scale. Now, write your final answer on the Health Maintenance Dial under the words "nutritional diet". For example, yes/8. (If you do not want to write in the book make a copy.)

Now proceed clockwise around the H.M.D.; point to "proper breathing" and ask: "At this time is John Doe breathing properly?" Write down your final answer, No/4.

Point your finger as you continue around the dial asking: "At this time is John Doe getting restful sleep?" "At this time is John Doe practicing toxic hygiene?" "At this time is John Doe getting enough relaxation?"

Now look for the no answers. Proper breathing and restful sleep received no answers. Appendix 1 on page 151 has extensive lists for each health maintenance area suggesting possible balancing alternatives. In order to maintain your health you need to restore equilibrium.

"Proper breathing" received a No/4. What could be the problem? What are some possible solutions? Here is a list that may suggest specific avenues of questioning.

Proper Breathing List

1. Air Quality
2. Allergy
3.. Smoking
4. Smokers
5. Shallow breathing
6. Rhythmic breathing
7. The Full Breath
8. Chest Cold
9. Lung Disorder
10. Lack of Air Circulation
11. Negative Ion Generation
12. The Mountains
13. Waterfalls
14. The Ocean
15. Pine Forest
16. Lack of Excercise
17. Etc.

The etcetera at the bottom of the list indicates there are many more possibilities left out, not known at this time, etc.

The H.M.D. tells you where you are and are not maintaining health. In addition, it tells you, at any given time, what your overall health maintenance level is.

If John Doe received tens in all six areas he would be in perfect health at 60. In fact, John Doe's health maintenance total was 37. A person's health maintenance level can be placed as follows:

Health Maintenance Level

60	=	Perfect
50-59	=	Excellent
35-49	=	Good
20-34	=	Poor
19-Below	=	Sickness, Disease, Illness, Dying, Death

With a 37, John Doe's health maintenance level falls toward the lower end of the "good" range. This would clearly indicate a conscientious effort is necessary to improve the health maintenance level.

The Long Road Ahead

Before going much further let's get it out in the open. Let's tell it like it is. Medical science as it stands does not condone, agree, endorse or even consider possible "medical pendulumology". Sure, there are physicians in the New Age underground who are successfully incorporating the pendulum into their traditional medical practice. Let's face it, though, they are few and far between, at least in the United States.

So, before I go on I want to tell you how I feel about the pendulum in health and healing. Based on my limited experience with friends and family I see the pendulum being used more and more in the healing arts. Naturally, it is years and years away from general use. Still, the seeds have been planted; the harvest will come in its season.

The methods introduced in this chapter are meant only as suggestions, possibilities and avenues for further research. I know there is a long road ahead. The journey begins with the first step. The methods covered in this chapter are just a few of those first steps.

To rely solely on the pendulum for health information would be like trying to drive a car by asking the pendulum when to turn right and when to turn left. It would be the way of a fool. Let's keep our heads on straight. The pendulum has undreamed of potential in the health field. But let's be sure to differentiate between dreams and reality.

Dreams often do become reality. Edison dreamed of lighting up the world. He tested no less than 10,000 substances searching for a filament that would light up a bulb. Meticulous, painstaking research, experimentation and testing were required before his dream became reality.

I take a similar view when it comes to the practical use of the pendulum in health and healing. Much work, much time, much energy must be applied to this rich field of pendulum work before it can be a universally accepted health and healing tool.

The American Society of Dowsers' Board of Trustees issued a statement of policy alerting the membership to the importance of informing themselves about federal and state law before engaging in healing practices. The Society's three legal counsels unanimously advised the Board of Trustees to adopt a strict policy.

> *"Members of the society wishing to diagnose or heal are notified they do so not as members of ASD, but personally, and at their own risk, and subject to the interpretation of the laws of their own State and the Pure Food, Drug and Cosmetic Act, passed by the U.S. Congress, which makes it a felony to diagnose or heal without a license, and with the interstate use of an instrument or device."*

> *"Members who wish to write or talk on bodily diagnosis or treatment, on the other hand, are entitled to do so under the First Amendment to the U.S. Constitution, which guarantees them freedom of speech. In view of ASD's position, however, they may not hold themselves out, in so doing, as representing ASD in any way, but rather as presenting a personal position."*

I applaud the American Society Dowsers' level-headed approach to diagnosis and healing using the pendulum or other dowsing instrument. Aspiring and practicing pendulumists may want to consider taking a similar position.

Finding the Dis-ease Level

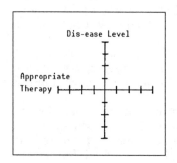

Figure 9: Dis-ease Level.

When a person's health maintenance level drops below 30 susceptibility to "dis-ease" increases dramatically. I purposely put quotes around and hyphenated the word "dis-ease". Dis-ease can simply be defined as a lack of ease. A disturbance somewhere in the physical-psychological-spiritual individual field has become sufficiently strong to be felt as a physiological problem.

Now, the source of the disturbance causing the dis-ease does not necessarily stem from the physical cellular level. Tuning-in with the pendulum it is possible to pinpoint the precise level from which the dis-ease is originating.

Finding the dis-ease level can be compared with a vertical axis. Choosing an appropriate therapy, which will be covered in the next section, can be compared to the horizontal axis. See Figure 9 above.

For clarity and simplicity I have divided the dis-ease levels into eight. In reality, each level can be divided into levels. The preciseness can be razor sharp. It's up to the pendulum practitioner to decide how precise they want to get.

The Eight Dis-ease Levels

1. Spiritual: Frequencies of Light, Love, Wisdom, Understanding, Strength, etc.
2. Etheric: Life energies entering this dimension through the force centers.
3. Mental: Word and image activities.
4. Feeling: Sensitivity to inner/outer events.
5. Emotional: Reactions like anger, anxiety, fear, impatience, etc.
6. Colloidal: The electrical activity across the cellular surfaces.
7. Chemical: The reactions/bonds between substances natural and toxic.
8. Cellular: The basic physiological unit that is ultimately affected by positive/negative activities on the various levels.

A pendulumist dowsing a dis-ease level may proceed as follows: "Is the source of John Doe's dis-ease spiritual? etheric? mental?, etc. A yes indicates the condition may originate mostly from that frequency level.

Health and medical professionals who have an affinity with the pendulum skill will find here a rich area of research. Diagnoses that have been made and verified through traditional means could be checked with the pendulum. Naturally, for control purposes, the readings should be done first then compared to the established diagnoses.

Choosing a Therapy

Once you have determined the dis-ease level (vertical) you can tune-in to the appropriate therapy (horizontal). During the transition time from the Piscean Age to the Aquarian Age, therapies are generally classified into two groups (1) medical and (2) wholistic.

The medical approach to treating dis-ease accepts as its initial premise that "dis-ease is physical", whatever that means. The wholistic approach, on the other hand, considers all the levels interconnected in the whole person.

It is my view that in the New Age "health maintenance" will be the new health profession integrating medical and wholistic therapies and treatments into one health maintenance science.

At present, generally speaking, medical practitioners scoff at the wholistic practices and wholistic practitioners push away medical doctors. Each practice, each therapy, whether medical or wholistic, has its specific beneficial use.

An aquaintance uses the pendulum to choose therapies for friends and family. He received a call asking to check the pendulum regarding the difficult passing of urine. It was not too hard to determine, even without the pendulum, that the fellow, being in his late fifties, had a prostrate problem.

My pendulum acquaintance proceeded to check possible appropriate therapies. He checked a long list of possible therapies all on the wholistic side - (see appendix 1 for therapy list).

Acupressure - 8, chiropractic adjustment - 7, cell salts - 7, the wholistic treatments mounted up. Still, not one reading came out 9 or 10.

Finally, the fellow suffered so much that his wife asked the pendulumist to check the use of a medical doctor. Instantly the pendulum rotated clockwise on 10. A list of doctors was quickly made up and checked. They called a highly rated physician.

Within a couple of weeks the man had successful minor surgery to correct the elimination difficulty. If he had not finally gone to the medical doctor who knows what would have happened. Apparently, toxins were backing up in his system. He was slowly poisoning himself to death.

I know of many more stories where a rigid wholistic mind-set blocked the appropriate use of medical treatment, and, of course, I could write volumes telling how people with medical mind-sets resisted the alternatives of wholistic therapies.

Here is just one. For about two months a friend suffered from low energy. It seemed to come on after a bout with the flu. It was all he could do to go to work and go home.

After exhausting traditional medical practices and his bank account, he turned to a wholistic oriental doctor. Only one visit was required to determine he had mild case of persistent hepatitis. A homeopathic remedy was prepared and given to my friend. His high energy level returned within two or three days.

Choosing the appropriate therapy is vital in New Age "Health Maintenance". Pain, suffering, death can be reduced and eliminated by tuning-in to the appropriate therapy for the level of dis-ease right at the beginning.

SUMMARY

1. The pendulum in health and healing is high touch in a high tech medical world. The pendulum is a kind of New Age stethoscope. It is one tool every health care specialist may eventually carry in their pocket.

2. In the long run maintaining your health at an optimum level will ward off sickness and dis-ease more than anything.

3. Health is a dynamic condition of physical, emotional, mental and spiritual balance which brings regenerating vitality to the cells, the instincts, the intellect and the intuition.

4. The Health Maintenance Dial focuses on the living physiological organism level. Taking care of your body affects your emotional, mental, and spiritual equilibrium as well. All these levels are interconnected and interrelated.

5. The methods introduced in this chapter are meant only as suggestions, possibilities and avenues for further research.

6. To rely solely on the pendulum for health information would be like trying to drive a car by asking the pendulum when to turn right and when to turn left.

7. The cause of a dis-ease does not necessarily stem from the physical/cellular level. Tuning-in with the pendulum, it is possible to pinpoint the precise level from which the dis-ease is originating.

8. It is my view that in the New Age "Health Maintenance" will be the new health profession integrating medical and wholistic therapies and treatments into one health maintenance science.

9. Choosing the appropriate therapy is vital in New Age "Health Maintenance". Pain, suffering, death and expense can be reduced and eliminated by tuning-in to the appropriate therapy for the level of dis-ease right at the beginning.

CHAPTER 10: FAMILY/DOMESTIC PENDULUM

The New Age Family

"The times, they are a changing"; the New Age is manifesting before our eyes, "for those who have eyes, let them see." The family structure is going through a radical change along with all the other traditional institutions.

Father, mother, brother, sister - these words used to have relatively fixed meanings; these roles had definite behaviors. Now things are different. Each individual must "define" their role based on "what is". In other words, fixed scripts do not work; individuals must see what is happening and adjust accordingly.

The New Age family is entering the energy world. Navigating the channels, bays and deep oceans of the energy world is best achieved by seeing what is, by direct perception - reception of the energy frequency.

During the age that is leaving us the father was the head of the family. The son was a chip off the old block; like father like son, John Doe Junior. The son should be a xerox copy of the father.

This mind-set goes against the energy world. During the New Age, family members are individuals first and family members second. An individual is conscious of energy; and an individual is conscious, to one degree or another, what energies they are radiating and what they are receiving.

As a result, labels like father and son take on a much more special meaning unique to each relationship. In other words father 1 is not father 2 is not father 3.... father n; son 1 is not son 2 is not son 3....son n; father-son relationship 1 is not father-son relationship 2, is not father-son relationship 3, etc.

Relationships are dynamic not static. The old age family relationships tend to be static; the New Age family relationships tend to be dynamic.

A New Age father does not necessarily have to be the blood father, Adoption, test tube babies, artificial insemination, genetic engineering, stepfathers and fathers as heads of groups have broken old age taboos - "my son must carry on the blood line".

In the New Age the blood line is less important - the genes, horizontal evolution. The level of being line is more important - the psychological/spiritual gene, the vertical evolution.

Carrying this tendency further leads to families forming according to the law of sympathetic vibration. Small groups (a form of the New Age family) are coming together, sharing, learning, exchanging and then, when the cycle is complete, separating.

The old age family tended to be fixed; the New Age family tends to be fluid.

The pendulum is a New Age tool. In the hand of a conscious, energy-oriented pendulumist the pendulum becomes a frequency world tuner. Direct perception, seeing and sensing what is becomes the way of New Agers.

In New Age family life the pendulum can assist the parents as well as the children in being more acutely aware of specific needs, wants, desires, problems and so on.

Food

From grocery shopping to the dinner table the pendulum can be used to measure the quality and quantity of your foods.

The shopping list you usually write up before going to the store becomes an excellent tool for dowsing foods. There are several ways the list can be utilized.

One

Go down the list asking this question - "On a 0 - 10 scale, what is the nutritional value of food x for my family? If you get a yes response below 7 then reconsider. Perhaps you should scratch it off the list.

Two

You can hold the pendulum over the entire list and ask: "does the cost of these groceries exceed my food budget?" A yes may alert you ahead of time to either bring more money or eliminate a few items.

Three

This question worded as follows: "will my family like and enjoy these foods?" Obviously, this is a general question. So, if you like, ask more specifically, "will so and so like and enjoy food x?" In the beginning, this specific questioning may be a bit tedious, but in the long run it will familiarize you with individual tastes.

Four

This one applies to the budget once again. "For the lowest price is Blank Grocery Store best?" You can check any number of stores. You may discover a 2 to 3 dollar overall savings per week at a store you have never shopped at.

No doubt there are many more ways of using your shopping list with the pendulum. Go ahead; discover the ways you find helpful.

Naturally, the list is not the food. Bring your pendulum to the store but use it at your own risk. On several occasions, I have brought out the pendulum at the grocery store. I try to use it discreetly but, alas, it does unleash some strange stares and unsettling vibrations.

The pendulum is particularly useful in the produce section to help pick out the best fruits and vegetables. Again, this procedure may be a bit risky unless there is no one in the store.

As an alternative, I "vib" the vegetables and fruits. It's a variation on the pendulum using your hand as the sensing, tuning tool. Pick up the produce you are considering. Hold it in your left hand, and cup your right hand and hold it over the item so that your finger tips can pick up the energy radiation quality from the fruit or vegetable.

Learning to "vib" may take some practice. It is less obvious than dowsing the produce but it is just as effective. After awhile you will pick up a definite energy current. It may feel "deep" and "soothing" - positive. Or it may feel "devitalizing" - negative. Practice; you will discover "vibing" is a great alternative to dowsing especially in public.

Planning a daily menu can be done more precisely with a pendulum. Make a list of the foods you have in mind for dinner: chicken, broccoli, boiled potatoes. Ask, "Is this combination of foods nutritional and enjoyable for my family?"

If you get a no, check out the items one by one. You may even want to take the food out of the refrigerator and hold the pendulum over each as you ask the question.

Again, in the beginning, planning menus for you and your family by tuning-in to the energy may take some time; but in the long run you will help your family to be nutritionally healthier and happier.

The pendulum can be used to find out the best way to cook a food. Frying, baking, broiling, steaming can be checked out. The length of time can be determined as well. Variations on recipes are easily tuned-in to: "if I put in a little more of such and such will it be pleasing to my family?"

Of course, ideally it is wise to check each family member individually for kinds of foods, ways and time of cooking, recipe variations, portions, etc. You could even keep a log on each person. No doubt certain individual likes, dislikes and nutritional needs would emerge.

In the old age, mother's intuition and feeling decided what was best for her family. In the New Age whoever prepares the meals needs intuition and direct tuning.

Too many foodstuffs today are polluted, poisons for profit. Most of us do not grow our own food. We buy it. Who knows where it is coming from and what it has gone through.

Tuning-in to the energy of food and beverages (check your water out) creates a higher level of consumer awareness. You do not have to read and believe the labels. You can experience directly the quality level of the food you purchase, cook and eat.

Clothing

How would you like to go to your closet and pick out the appropriate suit or outfit for work that day? You may have a special business meeting or sales call that could result in substantial dollars. Obviously, you must be prepared mentally and emotionally. But why not be prepared with the right clothing.

Most of us stand in front of the closet, take a look and pick out something to wear. If your intuition, sensitivity and feelings are keen then you are a pendulum. Most of us, though, could use improvement on the inner senses. Asking the pendulum the appropriate suit or outfit to wear that day could give you the extra percent needed to tilt the deal in your direction.

How to proceed? I personally like to choose color first and then the clothes. You may develop your own way of choosing clothes with the pendulum.

First, I write down a list of colors that are in my wardrobe:

Navy Blue
Tan
Dark Brown
Burgundy
Grey
Light Blue
White
Pink
Yellow
Red

Be sure to write down your own list based on what is in your closet. This list is by no means complete.

Next, go down the list asking this question: "On a 0 - 10 scale how wise is it for me to wear this color today?" A yes on the upper end of the scale indicates what color is appropriate that day.

Usually the color narrows the selection to a few possibilities. The next question is: "On a 0 - 10 scale, is this outfit appropriate to wear today?" Look at the outfit, the color; touch it. Sensing will tune you in more exactly.

You can apply the same line of pendulum questioning to important social events, family gatherings and athletic activities.

Clothes shopping can be a tedious and costly task. Many truly enjoy going from one store to the next searching for just the right sweater or pair of shoes.

If you are on a tight schedule and just do not have the time to wander from one store to the other, then take out your pendulum once again.

First, list the items of clothing you are looking for, for instance, a sweater and a pair of shoes. Second, write down the shopping malls in the area. Ask, "will I find the item I need at a price I can afford at x,y,z mall?"

Be even more specific if you want to spend even less time. For a pair of shoes, compile a list of shoe stores. Turning to the yellow pages is an excellent way to find a list already put together. Hold the pendulum over each shoe store display ad or listing and ask, "do they have the style and size shoes at a price I can afford?" Now find out how accurate your pendulum readings are.

Once you choose a clothing item for yourself or a family member you may want to double check the wisdom of the purchase before you hand over the cash. Most retail clothing stores have a change room where you can retreat for a quick final check. If you have any doubts go into neutral and tune-in. "Is it wise for me to purchase X at this time?"

Besides clothing you can check haircutters, haircuts, perfumes, cosmetics and jewelry. All areas of fashion and beauty can be dowsed to best serve your physical appearance needs.

Shelter

Choosing which apartment you are going to rent or house you are going to buy is most definitely a major life decision.

In the early 1970's I was living across the East River from Wall Street in Brooklyn Heights. It's a quaint, historic area of New York City with 100 to 200 year old brownstone walk-up apartment buildings.

I received a phone call from a close friend who just put a deposit on her dream apartment in Brooklyn Heights. The brownstone had been completely renovated. It had a fireplace, a skylight and a view of New York Harbor and the Statue of Liberty. Anyone would have thought, on first inspection, that her new apartment was indeed the dream apartment.

After moving in and getting settled, the negatives began to mount. In appearance the apartment was picture perfect. In reality, it caused her physical discomfort and many inconveniences.

First of all, the brownstone was close to a main truck route; eighteen wheelers driving by vibrated the building, a very uncomfortable feeling. In the winter the heat was inadequate because the back of the building was exposed to cold winds coming off the harbor.

There were many more negatives but the one that drove her from her dream apartment was the nightmare of cockroaches in the kitchen. She was so disgusted that she moved out before her lease ran out.

Tuning-in to the apartment with the pendulum, checking the compatibility with my friend and reviewing a list of positives and negatives could have saved her the aggravation and hundreds of dollars.

I have used this question for myself and friends: "on a 0 - 10 scale, all things considered, how wise is it for me to live at (address)?" Give a specific address. A nine or ten indicate a positive place to live.

The energy compatibility between you, your family and the apartment or house can also be checked "on a 0 - 10 scale what is the energy compatibility between me and (address)?" Give the exact address. Be sure to ask the compatibility level with each person who is going to be living at that address.

Everyone's energy field is different. Every apartment or home's energy field is different. Some energy patterns harmonize, others create discord.

A third way to dowse an apartment or house is to create a check list and pendulum out each factor on a 0 - 10 scale. Here is a partial list. Develop it further to suit your circumstances.

Monthly Payment	Landlord	Air Conditioning
Maintenance	Rent Increases	Neighbors
Noise Level	Sunshine	Major Appliances
View	Insulation	New Construction
Electrical Outlets	Heat	Schools
Hot Water	Shopping	Parking

The Kids

When it comes to your children the pendulum can be a godsend. Sometimes the lines of communication are down. We are unaware of their feelings, thoughts and concerns.

When you are not sure of what they are going through and are unable to talk openly, the pendulum may be the answer. A parent has an obligation to be aware of what their kids are going through. Superficial hellos and goodbyes fall far short of what is needed, loving communications.

Kids today as compared to kids even 15 or 20 years ago are exposed to so much more. Pay television, videos, sex, drugs, violence, crime, divorce, the list goes on.

Kids growing up today compared to kids growing up one hundred years ago live the equivalent of ten lifetimes by 30. The experience intensity when compared to the farm life of the 1880's is mind-boggling. Growing up in the 1980's and 1990's is an initiation, a trial by fire, a struggle for sanity. The environmental and psychic forces kids have to handle today take determination, strength and spiritual fortitude.

As parents, we are the guides. When our sight fails us the pendulum can be used to see beyond the physical senses. It's potential use in raising the kids is limitless. You will discover many more applications than I will sketch here.

How do you know how much time would be wise for your son or daughter to spend on homework? First, determine the best time in the evening for each child. Then, find out the total amount of time for all subjects. And, finally, determine the time length for each subject.

You may want to word the questions as follows: "All things considered what is the best time in the evening for homework - for John?; 5:00, 5:30, 6:00, 6:30", etc., until you get a positive rotation. "How long would it be wise for John to spend on homework tonight? 1 hour, 1 1/2 hours, 2 hours", etc. "How long would it be wise for John to spend studying math, english, history?, etc.; 1/2 hour, 3/4 hour, 1 hour, etc.

If you are fairly accurate with the pendulum then the time framework will be extremely helpful to your children. Naturally, you must take into consideration your childrens' likes, dislikes, needs and energy level. The word "wise" refers to the overall relationship between your child and their homework.

Television, video and movies can be a perplexing area for parents. What is good and what is bad? What is right and what is wrong? From an energy world, frequency universe view there is no black and white.

Getting caught in the opposites - what is called in general semantics the two-valued orientation - leads to confusions, contradictions and hypocrisy.

In the frequency universe there is, at any given moment, degrees of harmonious to inharmonious vibrations relative to a particular person. So when you ask the pendulum, "Is it wise for John to watch X TV show, video or movie?", you really are tuning to the energy level.

In other words, what everybody is saying is not good for children may, from the energy level, be perfect for your child. And the reverse may be true; what everybody is saying is great for kids may be totally negative for your son or daughter.

Raising your kids with an extra-perceptive sense, which the pendulum helps you in developing, will perhaps give them the extra boost needed to navigate daily life obstacles.

Recreation

Family vacations and outings can be a joy or a misery. The pendulum helps you choose the joys and eliminate the miseries.

Picnics, reunions, family gatherings, drives in the country - there is so much families can do together. With everyone busy with different activities, the family fun must be selective. Nobody wants a miserable experience.

Let's say this coming Saturday the whole family is going on a picnic. Where to go? Make a list of your favorite picnic spots or take out a map of the area.

Now you are ready to check the pendulum. The question: "On a 0 - 10 scale is X the best picnic spot for the family on Saturday?" As you may have noticed this is a future question. Answers to future questions can be a little tricky. I would suggest, then, you double check first thing Saturday morning to confirm which picnic areas receive the highest mark. You can even ask what time to arrive in order to have a picnic table and barbeque pit.

Literally any family activity can be tuned-in to. Skiing families may wake up early Saturday morning and check the pendulum to find out which area has the best conditions and will not be overcrowded. Gather brochures, ask everybody where they would like to go, find out prices, set a budget then take out the pendulum. Again, we are dealing with a future question; that's why the fact gathering stage is helpful. It gives you more to go on.

I have found wording a future question as follows improves the accuracy: "Based on the way things are going now, what is the percent possibility of the whole family enjoying a vacation to X?"

Now we are using a 0 - 100 percent scale. Begin with 90 - 100 and work your way down the scale in intervals of 10, until you get a yes answer. Then, if you want to be even more precise, work your way up one by one until the pendulum gyrates clockwise.

Obviously, there is no guarantee. Life's dynamic not static. The future is fluid, not yet crystalized. Still, 90% plus readings indicate a high possibility of family fun.

Family recreational activities are an excellent area to dowse. Make a list; here is a sample list that may get you started:

Hiking	Racketball
Biking	Touch Football
Swimming	Basketball
Ice Skating	Jogging
Skiing	Volleyball
Tennis	Handball

Finding and participating in activities for the whole family will bring you closer. Shared experiences balance the day to day living pressures, conflict and tensions that inevitably happen between people who live together.

SUMMARY

1. The New Age family is entering the energy world. Navigating the channels, bays and deep oceans of the energy world is best achieved by seeing what is, by direct perception - reception of the energy frequency.

2. During the New Age, family members are individuals first and family members second. An individual is conscious, to one degree or another, what energies they are radiating and what they are receiving.

3. Relationships are dynamic not static. The old age family relationships tended to be static; the new age family relationships tend to be dynamic.

4. The penduum is a New Age tool. In the hand of a conscious, energy - oriented pendulumist, the pendulum becomes a frequency world tuner. Direct perception, seeing and sensing what is, becomes the way of New Agers.

5. In New Age family life the pendulum can assist the parents as well as the children in being more acutely aware of specific needs, wants, desires, problems and so on.

6. From grocery shopping to the dinner table the pendulum can be used to measure the quality and quantity of your foods.

7. As an alternative to the pendulum at the produce section of the grocery store, "vib" the vegetables and fruits. It's a variation on the pendulum, using your hand as the sensing, tuning tool.

8. With the pendulum you do not have to read and believe the labels. You can experience directly the quality level of the food you purchase, cook and eat.

9. Asking the pendulum the appropriate suit or outfit to wear on any given day could give you the extra percent needed to tilt the deal in your direction.

10. Besides clothing you can check haircutters, haircuts, perfumes, cosmetics and jewelry. All areas of fashion and beauty can be dowsed to best serve your physical appearance needs.

11. Tuning-in to the apartment with the pendulum, checking the compatibility with my friend and reviewing a list of positives and negatives, could have saved her the aggravation and hundreds of dollars.

12. Everyone's energy field is different. Every apartment or home's energy field is different. Some energy patterns harmonize, others create discord.

13. When you are not sure what your kids are going through and are unable to talk openly the pendulum may be the answer.

14. Raising your kids with an extra-perceptive sense, which the pendulum helps you in developing, will, perhaps, give them the extra boost needed to navigate daily life obstacles.

15. Family vacations and outings can be a joy or misery. The pendulum helps you choose the joys and eliminate the miseries.

CHAPTER 11: TIPS, HINTS, POINTERS

Choosing a Pendulum

There are literally thousands of different pendulums. A shop in Paris is purported to have over one thousand pendulums on display. Choosing a pendulum that is just right for you can be exasperating.

Two of my pendulumist friends told me how they found the right pendulum for them.

Don was using a pencil pendulum. It was made of a sharpened #2 pencil tangling from a string. He attached a dowel horizontal to the pencil as a handle.

Although the pencil pendulum served its purpose, he decided to find a pendulum that would be just right for him. He asked, "is it wise for me to find and make my own pendulum"? Answer: Yes.

He continued his search for a pendulum by asking "is it wise for me to construct a pendulum from wood". Answer: Yes. "Is it wise for me to construct a pendulum from oak?" Answer: No. "Is it wise for me to make it out of ash?" Answer: Yes.

He narrowed down the field of choices further by pinpointing a certain woods in the area where the best ash tree for his pendulum would be located. He drove to the area, got out of the car and walked into the woods.

Tree by tree (ash trees only) he asked: "would a branch from this tree be best for my pendulum?" Finally, he received a "yes" answer. Next, he proceeded to ask which branch would make the best pendulum for him.

Don left with his prized ash branch. He returned home where he designed and fashioned a perfect pendulum for him. Much of the pendulum still has the original bark on it. It's a beauty.

When I asked him about the difference between his pencil pendulum and his handmade ash pendulum he answered, "it's the difference between night and day. My ash pendulum responds quickly and accurately."

Larry's story goes something like this. Larry attended a meeting of his local chapter of the American Society of Dowsers.

At the time he was a beginner eager to learn all he could about the pendulum and dowsing. When the meeting was over one of the group leaders pointed to a table with about a hundred small crystals on it.

He said to the group, "we have dowsed these crystals and have found them to be good for dowsing. If you need a pendulum come on up and pick one out."

Larry wasted no time. He needed a pendulum. He glanced down at the table scanning the variety of shapes, sizes, colors and textures. When a crystal appealed to him he picked it up. He held it, checking out his feelings.

After about six or seven tries he was attracted to a small pink crystal. He picked it up. That was it. He felt tingling sensations in his hand and fingers. The crystal was warm. Larry had found his pendulum.

What am I saying? No one pendulum is the best for everyone. You will know which pendulum responds best for you. It does not have to be expensive or fancy.

On the other hand if you are attracted to an expensive pendulum, it responds instantly for you and you can afford it, by all means buy it.

Another area to consider is different pendulums for different types of dowsing. One may be better for detecting precious metals another for picking up on psychic vibrations. This is a rich area of research as long as we keep our sights on the fact that you and I are the pendulum. We must avoid making the tool more important than consciousness.

Pendulum Care

Just as a carpenter, electrician, gardener or plumber respects and takes special care of his tools so must the pendulumist. Your pendulum is your intuitive antenna. Taking good care of it means better reception of answers.

Keeping your pendulum in a safe and special place will help to maintain your vibrations on, in and through the pendulum. Some pendulumists return their tuning tool to the same place each time they are done. Others store their pendulum in a small pouch and carry it in their pocket or purse.

Some pendulumists store their pendulum inside a miniature pyramid. A small pyramid when properly constructed and aligned north-south acts as a resonator and condenser of cosmic energy. The force-field of energy surrounding and interpenetrating your pendulum will receive an extra charge. In addition, the molecules will tend to align giving your pendulum a more powerful feel; it will seem alive when you hold it.

Most pendulumists are particular about who handles or touches their pendulum. Ever notice a musician's attitude about just anybody picking up their guitar or horn? That's a no-no. Pendulumists are very much the same way.

The revelations of Kirlian photography partly explains what is behind the "please do not touch" feeling. Researchers have taken Kirlian photographs of objects before and after someone has touched or handled it. There is a definite difference. The object radiates different colors before and after.

I had a recent conversation with an electrical consultant for Westinghouse who indicated infrared scan devices can detect the presence of different heat sources. Apparently, every living person, place and thing radiates heat uniquely. Your heat radiation is like your thumbprint; no one else is the same.

He went on to tell me that the latest security systems utilize infrared scans connected to a computer. If the person's heat radiation does not match the stored memory of their unique pattern a security officer is automatically summoned to that location. The electrical consultant went on to tell me that even plastic surgery will not stop infrared scan detection.

So, when someone touches your pendulum it changes its vibration. Depending on who touches it, a positive or negative person, it could throw off your readings.

Inaccurate Pendulum: Why?

The number one reason for inaccurate pendulum readings, that I have noticed to date, is vague and faulty wording of the question. Review chapters four and five to see whether or not you are wording your questions specifically and precisely.

"Is John a good boy" is a vague and faulty type of question. Your accuracy with the pendulum will be minimal if you fall into this bad habit. An example of a more specific question about John might be "did John get an "A" on his spelling test today?" Do you see the difference?

The number two reason for inaccurate pendulum readings is your psychological state when you do the reading. I might add that reason number two is a close second. In fact, it may be more accurate for me to say that "wording the question" and "your psychological state" are two sides of the number one reason for pendulum inaccuracies.

What do I mean by psychological state? While you word, ask the question and hold the pendulum out, you are in a mental-emotional-physical state. Are you aware of thoughts, emotions, excess tensions? This is your psychological state.

The vibrations from your psychological condition can very much effect the rotation of the pendulum. Here's a dramatic example. A gifted pendulumist friend dazzles you with his accuracy, about 75 - 85%. In one area his accuracy to date has been zero.

When he is asked to check the sex of a fetus he is inevitably wrong. He discovered why: it seems all his life he has resisted having children. He gets uptight at the thought of becoming a father.

So you see, my friend's psychological state at the point of reading distorts the clear reception of the answer. Once you word questions specifically, then a high percentage of inaccuracy is a result of subconscious blocks, attitudes and desires distorting or altering the answer.

Another prominent source of pendulum inaccuracy is the lack of patience. I know of a person who has marveled at my pendulum use for years. I usually say, "practice makes perfect." They respond by trying it two or three times and then giving up. They lack patience.

You must take a detached, patient approach to the pendulum. When you ask a question concern about "right" and "wrong", whatever they mean, if anything, interferes with clear reception.

In the beginning wanting to be an expert creates impatience. In turn, the impatience creates inaccuracy, discouragement, failure; you give up.

Instead, approach the pendulum one day at a time. Watch, wait, see and try again. Gradually, your confidence will build. Your questions will be more precise. You will notice your psychological states and adjust them when necessary.

If you find your mind wandering while you ask the question and wait for the answer, your concentration may be lacking. What does it mean to concentrate? The word concentrate can be divided into con - centrate meaning con - with, and centrate - center. To concentrate means "with center".

To be at attention, to be aware here-now is to be "with center", centered in a state of concentration.

The wandering mind creates interference patterns in your auric-field. Chances are, then, that whatever rotation the pendulum takes will be distorted.

How do you develop the necessary concentration? Choose five or six objects, place them on a table, sit down and begin observing them. Observe without associating, without thinking, without memories. Practice looking at the shape, the color, the form, the design; touch - feel the texture and shape.

Practice this exercise daily. Strengthen your concentration muscle. Eventually, you will steady your mind. You should be able to hold your attention steady during the length of a reading. Concentration will increase your accuracy.

Pendulum Misuses

There is a tendency to consult the pendulum every time you or another has a question. At that point the pendulum stops being a tool for cultivating intuitive perception and starts becoming a mental-emotional-spiritual crutch.

When you make an oracle of the pendulum you abdicate a certain degree of your "center" of your "being" to an external object, process or system.

Now, if every time you had a question, you pulled out the pendulum you certainly would be a sorry sight, and a funny one too. Let's say you want to know how to get to a friend's house. Instead of asking the pendulum, call your friend up, ask for the directions and write them down.

Do you want to know the time? Ask the pendulum. It is possible to use the pendulum to find out the time. But it is a lot easier to look at a watch or clock.

Remember - you are a pendulum. Everything you do with the pendulum you can do without it. In other words, you can tune-in without holding the pendulum in front of you; ask and ye shall receive.

There are times when tuning-in must be done quickly and accurately; it could be a matter of life or death. Living in New York City there were times when I had to walk alone on dark streets at night or wait on subway platforms with no one else around.

Sometimes I felt twinges of apprehension in the belly. To counteract the apprehension I tuned-in to see where I should walk or stand. I might ask this question mentally, "Is it wise for me to walk on this side of the street?" If a "No" popped into my mental awareness I would take a different route.

Once your perceptive and intuitive awareness have become clear, then even taking time to ask a question mentally may be too slow, especially in a life or death situation. A strong awareness knows ahead of time what to do or not do.

Making an oracle of the pendulum is a misuse. Use the pendulum wisely to develop awareness, perception and intuition. These skills of consciousness are within and only need to be brought out through repeated use. The pendulum is only one way to help bring it out.

Another pendulum misuse is what I call "psychic prying". Once you become accurate with the pendulum you discover the possibility that all frequencies are available for tuning. You begin to feel that if you need to know something you simply tune-in and the answer comes to you.

There is a temptation to satisfy every strong curiousity. In my opinion, a pendulumist must discriminate when and when not to ask the pendulum. Curiosity of a personal nature may be an indicator of "psychic prying".

To be more specific, let's say you are curious about the love life of a friend. Maybe you are attracted to her boyfriend and want to know if they are getting along. Do you see this is getting too personal?

On the other hand, if your friend asked you to check the pendulum in an effort to improve or understand the relationship your personal thoughts and feelings are not as involved.

Living in Reno, Nevada many people have asked me about gambling and the pendulum. Based on what I have seen and experienced to date, it appears gambling and the pendulum do not mix for four reasons.

First, the vibrations in a casino are intense, greedy, desperate and generally unbalanced. This factor alone almost guarantees a wrong answer.

Second, the casino management is not going to look too favorably on someone stopping to ask a question before taking another hit at a 21 table.

Third, your motivation is more than likely selfish greed, a frequency that blocks accuracy.

Fourth, many gambling questions are future questions like when picking a winning horse or selecting a slot machine that will jackpot. The future is plactic. One slight factor can alter the event completely. Even the fact that you ask about the future alters the possible event you are asking about.

Occult Associations

Many times over the years, I have met people who have negative "occult" association with any mention of the pendulum. Usually the association is with the ouija board. What's your automatic association with the ouija board? Is it seances, calling on the departed, black magic?

Recently, at a local New Age bookstore I gave a talk titled, "You are a Pendulum", outlining many of the points presented in this book. I clearly indicated that the pendulum is only one tool of many which can be used by some to improve perceptive and intuitive awareness. I brought up nothing of an "occult" nature like tarot, astrology, psychic phenomenon, etc. In fact, as much as possible, I used scientific language to explain how the pendulum worked.

Still, after the talk, a woman came up to me and said, "I enjoyed what you had to say, except the pendulum is too occult, too much like the ouija board."

I replied, "the way I see it, at this time, a person's level of being determines the level of pendulum use. The world's most spiritual philosophy can be corrupted by a selfishly motivated individual."

It is unfortunate but true that the misuse of the so called occult arts has been covered extensively by newspapers, television and the movies. Sensationalism sells. Those who misuse have tainted the reputations of those who use wisely and for the benefit of others.

The associations people have with the sound of the word "occult" are changing as the level of consciousness changes in our society. The dictionary defines occult as follows: of or relating to supernatural influences, agencies or phenomena; beyond human comprehension; available only to the initiate, secret.

If you break the word down to its roots you have oc meaning eight, like in octave, and cult, the root of culture. So occult's root meaning is the eight-fold culturing. This implies a well rounded, whole person development. It implies balance as opposed to negative psychism.

Anyway, as a pendulumist it is important you are aware of the strong negative occult reaction you may get from some. Taking it personally will achieve little. Understanding will help keep the communication lines open.

Advanced Readings

So far, I have stayed pretty much with the yes/no reading and the 0 - 10 scale reading. I have used several other kinds of readings.

Asking a question once can be detrimental to accuracy. When there's a difficult question in the area of health, business or personal relationship doing a "wide angle reading" or "synthesis reading" may give you more and clearer information.

I define a wide angle reading as the repetition of the same question at several different times. You then take the consensus of all the readings as the answer to a particular question.

Say you have an opportunity to change jobs with a substantial pay increase but you must relocate to a new city. Naturally, you first gather all the relevant information like how much, how soon, what is the new city's environment?, etc.

Next, you decide to check the pendulum. You form the question. It may read, "on a 0 - 10 scale how wise is it for my overall life experience to accept a job with X, Y, Z, Company in New York?" Be sure to date the question; indicate the time if you are doing several readings in a day.

Over two or three days you may have seven or eight readings, mostly eights and nines. I would interpret that to mean it is an excellent opportunity, but realize ahead of time it is by no means perfect.

I know a pendulumist who was offered a part-time disc jockey position at a local radio station. His first emotional reaction was to forget it. He was already extremely busy in his business. Still, he checked the pendulum. He got a nine.

Over the next week he did a wide angle reading; he asked the same question fifteen or twenty times. He consistently received nines. He realized if the pendulum had any validity he best take the job despite his disinterest.

During the next twelve months a host of positives resulted from his part-time announcing. He overcame more of his public speaking fear. He earned substantial fees for writing radio commercials. He made some excellent connections and contacts. He met his future business associate. Actually, the list goes on and on.

Sometimes when I think of this incident it staggers my mind. I wonder how often we push away, because of an automatic dislike, the very event, person or thing that could dramatically change our life for the best.

When I ask a number of different questions about a person, a situation, a place, a thing, etc. I call it a "synthesis reading". An example of a synthesis reading on a person would be the "Eight-Spoked Wheel of Whole Living" presented in Chapter Six: The Well-Rounded Pendulumist.

Say for instance, you cannot make up your mind which direction to expand your business in. Every time you take a look you see 5 or 6 options. What to do? Do a synthesis reading.

If you are in the restaurant business you may write out the following questions. On a 0 - 10 scale:

1. Would it be wise to open a second restaurant?

2. How wise would it be for us to build on to the present restaurant?

3. Would it be wise to redecorate the present restaurant?

4. Would it be wise to add a bar to the restaurant?

5. How wise would it be to create and print new menus?

6. When would it be wise to open for business?

Anyway, as you can plainly see, the questions go on and on. Gradually, it becomes clear what direction it would be wise to take. In a way, it is like putting together a jig-saw puzzle. At first, you have no idea what the picture looks like; but as you put more pieces together the picture becomes clearer and clearer.

SUMMARY

1. No one pendulum is the best for everyone. You will know which pendulum responds best for you.

2. As long as we keep our sights on the fact that you and I are the pendulum, we avoid making the tool more important than the consciousness behind it.

3. Just as a carpenter, electrician, gardener or plumber respects and takes special care of his tools so must the pendulumist. Your pendulum is your intuitive antenna. Taking good care of it means better reception of answers.

4. Keeping your pendulum in a safe and special place will help to maintain your vibrations on, in and through the pendulum.

5. Pendulumists are usually particular about who handles or touches their pendulum. When someone touches your pendulum it changes its vibration. Depending on who touches it, a positive or negative person, it could throw off your readings.

6. The number one reason for inaccurate pendulum readings is vague and faulty wording of the question.

7. The number two reason is your psychological state, the thoughts, emotions, feelings, images, desires, hopes, wishes, etc., that vibrate in and through your psyche.

8. A third source of pendulum inaccuracy is a lack of patience. Approach the pendulum one day at a time. Watch, wait, see and try again.

9. Inaccuracy occurs when there is a lack of concentration. Practice concentrating until you are able to hold your attention steady during the length of the reading.

10. There is a tendency to consult the pendulum every time you or another has a question. At that point the pendulum stops being a tool for cultivating intuitive perception and starts becoming a mental-emotional-spiritual crutch.

11. Making an oracle of the pendulum is a misuse. Use the pendulum wisely to develop awareness, perception and intuition. These skills of consciousness are within and only need to be brought out through repeated use. The pendulum is only one way to help bring them out.

12. In my opinion, a pendulumist must discriminate when and when not to ask the pendulum. Curiosity of a personal nature may be an indicator of "psychic prying".

13. It is wise to be aware of the "negative occult" reaction you may get from some toward the pendulum. Taking it personally will achieve little. Understanding will possibly keep the communication lines open.

14. A wide angle reading is the repetition of the same question at several different times. You then take the consensus of all the readings as the answer to a particular question.

15. A number of different questions about a person, a situation, a place, a thing, etc., is called a synthesis reading.

CHARACTER ANALYSIS CHART

PATIENCE	
UNDERSTANDING	
WISDOM	
KNOWLEDGE	
LOVE	
CONSCIOUSNESS	
CONCENTRATION	
SENSE OF HUMOR	
ARTISTIC ABILITY	
MUSICAL ABILITY	
WRITING ABILITY	
BUSINESS ABILITY	
PHYSICAL FITNESS	
LEADERSHIP	
SOCIABILITY	
COOPERATION	
INTEGRITY	
SELF-CONFIDENCE	
FLEXIBILITY	
DETERMINATION	
INTUITION	
IMAGINATION	
SENSITIVITY	
FEAR	
DECISIVENESS	

Figure 10: Character Analysis
Chart.

CHAPTER 12: PSYCHOLOGICAL PENDULUM

Character Analysis

Have you ever taken a test to determine your talents, strengths and, yes, weaknesses. Somewhere along the way we have all taken so called aptitude tests. Psychologists are generally agreed, knowing where you stand is much better than not knowing.

With the pendulum there is no need for tedious, stressful, time consuming and costly testing. Energy is real; it can be registered and felt. Our character traits emanate a vibration whether actual or potential.

With the pendulum you can eliminate weeks, months and even years of psychological counseling by asking a few questions. Too often psychologists are hung up on all kinds of intellectual theory that, in the long run, do nothing more than confuse.

Tuning to energy is clear and simple, you register, feel, experience. You know directly the talents, strengths and weaknesses. There is no need to guess, suspect, suppose or speculate. A character analysis with the pendulum is quick, accurate and inexpensive.

So, how do you proceed? Look at Figure 10, Character Analysis Chart on page 113.

Hold the pendulum over each trait and ask: on a 0 - 10 scale how balanced is John Doe's (fill in the trait)? Descending from 10 - 0 ask: is John Doe's (fill in the trait) - 10? Continue until you get a yes answer. Proceed in the same way through each section.

Often, when I have done these character analysis readings, new and unexpected information comes to light. It is amazing to me how little we really know ourselves.

I have gotten 8s, 9s and 10s on musical ability for people who do not even sing, play an instrument or listen to music. I recall a woman who had a 10 reading on singing ability. She had not done any steady singing for twenty-five years. She suffered from regular sore throats, frustration and other emotional problems. After her character analysis reading, she decided to join a local choir. The positive change in her character is astounding since rediscovering the joys of singing.

As you work through the Character Analysis Chart write your answers down next to each trait. Be sure to indicate the date of the reading. You may want to re-do the pendulum character analysis at a later date. This can be particularly helpful if you have worked on some weak points in your character and you want to see if there has been some progress.

By the way, for those of you who recall Chapter 5: Semantic Pendulum, you may want to be sure you know what you mean by some of the traits listed.

Love, understanding and wisdom are referred to in General Semantics as high order abstractions. Simply stated - they are mouthfuls! We often do not really know what we mean when we say them.

For instance, there are many levels of love. When you ask on a 0 - 10 scale how much "love" does (name) radiate? What do you mean? When I ask that question I mean something like: the impersonal giving energy that expects nothing in return and gives for the joy of giving. Based on the way you act, what is your referent for the word "love".

Doing character analysis readings will lead to self-knowledge and insight into your character and the character of others.

Psychologists would find the pendulum a remarkable, productive and effective addition to their practice. The psychologist capable with the pendulum can know a lot about a client before meeting them for the first time. Direct perception and experience is more immediate and accurate than intellectual analysis of so called complexes.

Subconscious Blockages

The subconscious layer of consciousness is not "sub", beneath, below, lower. Rather, it is simply a different nature or structure. With this point clear I will continue to use the word subconscious.

The nature of the subconscious is to reflect and retain. When wonderful things are happening they are reflected and retained by the subconscious. The subconscious then reacts like a positive feedback circuit giving you constructive feelings about whatever you are going to do.

Unfortunately, most of us have not lived charmed lives. To keep things interesting negative events have been reflected and retained by the subconscious. Now, when a particular negative event is repeated over and over, or had an exceptionally powerful impact, we experience a subconscious blockage.

A subconscious blockage is a crystalization of life energy which interferes with the natural flow of events in that area of life. Take a look at the **Circle of Subconscious Blockages**, Figure 11 on page 116.

Let's take a for instance, section one, self-image. Have you known anyone with a bad self-image? They usually feel incapable of accomplishing certain tasks. Usually they talk about themselves in a negative way. "I'm not good enough." "I can't do it."

When the subconscious reflects and retains a poor self-image a person becomes powerless to achieve most anything. The life energy locked up in the subconscious needs to be released.

There are many, many ways of releasing subconscious blocked energies, each more or less effective depending on the person. But before I pass along a few methods, I want to show you how to dowse subconscious blockages.

Starting with Section One, self-image, personality, physical appearance, ask the following question: on a 0 - 10 scale how balanced is the life energy flow in this subconscious area? Be sure to focus your awareness on the words in that section of the subconscious wheel.

Proceeding from 10 to 0 the degree of balance or unbalance. Write the number you get next to each section. Continue around the wheel. Note where there is the most and least balance. Readings of 0 - 6 could use some work.

Now some easy exercises for releasing subconscious blockages:

1. Take a pad of paper and a pen, sit down at a table or desk and begin writing anything and everything that comes to mind about that life area. Write intensely. Scribble if you need to. When done, do not read it. Tear it up and throw it away.

2. Sit down in a quiet room. In the mind's eye review in a detached way your personal history in that life area. Observe coolly. See without reacting.

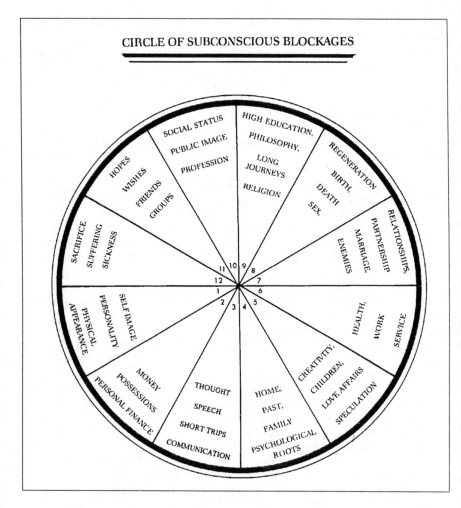

Figure 11: Circle of Subconscious Blockages.

3. Become acutely conscious of thoughts, feelings, emotions and attitudes in an unbalanced area. Be conscious. Analysis and extensive thinking are taboo. Simply be conscious and then register without reacting.

The Family Force-Field

I watched a documentary on public television recently about a Venezuelan family. This 3,000 strong family had a history of Hungtington's disease; it effects a specific area of the brain with resultant lack of muscular control. Each family member carried a gene pattern that, when activated, brought on Hungtington's disease.

Besides genetic family patterns there are psychological family patterns. And just as the Venezuelan family has carried Hungtington disease down the generations there are family psychological patterns carried down the generations. I call the psychological energy patterns the family force-field.

A high school friend, who I'll call Sam, was chained mightily to his family force-field. For years his individual goals, desires and objectives were swept aside by the power of the family force-field.

At 21, he was in love but not ready to marry. His family interfered. Living together was out of the question, he must marry.

Sam went into the family business against his will. Instead of pursuing his interest in electronics he fell into the family pattern of working in the plumbing business.

Example after example could be given of how the family patterns superceded Sam's individual desires. The pendulum can be used to detect family patterns. Becoming conscious of these patterns is the first step toward breaking their hold.

Ask this question: what percent of (name) psychological energies are identified with family patterns? Then ask 90 - 100%, 80 - 90%, 70 - 80%, etc., until you get a positive rotation from the pendulum.

Now, once you determine the degree of identification find out which parent has the most influence. A simple yes/no question - does the mother have the greater influence? If yes, it's the mother; if no, the father.

Someone with the determination and will to "find their own center", "become their own person", "to be an individual" must now observe the more influential parent and notice those traits which they have identified with, both positive and negative.

Next, there must be a decision about what traits are helpful in becoming an individual and which traits are harmful. The harmful traits must be eliminated. This is achieved by non-identification. The critical moment of identification must be altered by detachment.

The conscious act of detachment stops the flow of life energy into the disagreeable family pattern. Without energy the pattern will disintegrate. It will no longer affect the individual force-field.

Frequencies of the Race Psyche

Sometimes a family pattern can also be a race psyche pattern. Or a personality pattern can be directly from the Frequencies Of the Race Psyche (F.O.R.P.).

Cultures and nationalities exhibit different psychological traits. When I traveled to Europe some years ago no one mistook me for an Englishman. Most knew I was American. Rarely, if ever, did I mistake an Englishman for an American.

Cultures and nationalities have built up FORPS which most people in a race psyche reflect in their personalities to one degree or another. What happens when a individual's psychological nature does not mesh with his or her race psyche? Many of the same conflicts and frustrations take place as occur between the individual and the family force-field

Around 1980 a high ranking Soviet official secretly defected to the United States. He was asked why he did it. He replied, "in the Soviet Union you cannot speak openly about what you are thinking, not even with your own family. Everything is a lie. You are constantly on the defense to say what you are supposed to say.

"In the United States you say what's on your mind to friends, family, strangers and even in the public media. I could not stand the oppression anymore."

This high ranking government official left his wife, children and friends. He agreed to be a spy for the C.I.A. to prove his loyalty. He gave up everything to break the destructive hold of one race psyche to follow his individual inclinations.

Using the pendulum you can easily determine the strength of identification a person has with any given race psyche. Ask, "on a 0 - 100 % scale how identified is (name) with the (x) race psyche? 90 - 100%, 80 - 90%, 70 - 80%? Once you get a yes answer you can keep asking until you get the exact degree.

Naturally, if someone is more or less comfortable and content with their present life situation there is no need to find out the sources of pain, conflict and frustration. On the other hand, if life has become an unbearable series of conflicts then it may be time to track down the sources of difficulty.

The pendulum psychologist bypasses the verbal, the theoretical, the intellectual and tunes-feels-experiences directly the energies, frequencies and forces frustrating an individual's natural growth.

Practice observing the FORPS (Frequencies of the Race Psyche). Do you notice the obvious FORPS of the American Race Psyche. What do American's focus on most. What do other societies, nationalities and cultures focus on? What a race psyche focuses on builds up patterns of group behavior.

When certain race psyche patterns go too much against a person's nature, as with the Soviet official's, then a person either suffers or lets go of the destructive FORPS.

Rapports

In the fall of 1977 I was walking with a woman friend in the Wall Street area of New York City. It was a Saturday and she was going to work at a large law firm. Once I walked her to work I was going to go to a New Age bookstore in Manhattan.

Anyway, she suddenly complained of sharp stabbing pains in her chest. Needless to say, she was very concerned. Since we were walking I could not check the pendulum for the pain source. So instead, knowing we are truly living pendulums, I tuned-in.

I immediately got an image of my friend's mother. The pains came and went several times. She definitely thought something was physically wrong with her.

I had only known her a few months so I hesitated to tell her that she was picking up a rapport - a negative sympathetic vibration - from her mother.

As we approached her work place she began getting distraught so I decided to say something.

"You're picking up a sympathetic vibration, a rapport from your mother," I said decisively.

She looked at me like I was crazy. "You mean to tell me you think this pain comes from my mother? Now I have heard everything.

"Don't believe me," I responded. Go to the telephone and call her. Ask her how she's doing."

"That's ridiculous" she said.

"It doesn't hurt to check it out, though, does it?" I prodded.

Anyway, she agreed to call her mother as soon as she sat down at her desk.

Later that afternoon I returned to pick her up. She had a flabbergasted look on her face.

"You know I called my mother and she was angry and upset. Also, right after I hung up the pains subsided and then went away."

The pendulum psychologist can track down the source of rapports. Becoming conscious of the source of a rapport usually cuts the connection between you and that source.

What are some of the symptoms of rapports? Slight stabbing pains in the chest, sudden headaches, gas attacks, heat in the back of the neck, a draining of life energy, etc.

Awareness is the key to handling rapports. At the instant you begin to pick up one of these negative vibrations do the following:

1. Register, do not react.
2. Go in neutral.
3. Stop identifying.
4. Begin slow rhythmic breathing through the nose.
5. Change the focus of attention.

The point is, you want to cut the flow of negative energy before the circuit/connection is completed.

Test out what I've said about rapports. Tune-in with the pendulum in order to track down the rapport source. Working with this process for a few months you will begin to sense a rapport and where it is coming from within seconds.

Percentage of Consciousness

Before measuring percentage of consciousness I must give a referent for consciousness. What do I mean by consciousness? Let me start by telling you what I do not mean.

By consciousness I do not mean the everyday waking consciousness that is aware of people, things and places. By consciousness I do not mean anything mystical, metaphysical or psychic.

By consciousness I do mean an acute, alert state of awareness which detects subtleties of energy, thought, feeling, etc. Now, there is a direct relationship between a person's degree of consciousness and their level of being. The lower the level of consciousness the less evolved the being. The greater the level of consciousness the more evolved the being.

Measuring degrees of consciousness with the pendulum can be quite startling at first, at least it was for me. I found out rather quickly that most people are not conscious. As a result, I was not only measuring degrees of consciousness but also degrees of unconsciousness.

Distinct differences between conscious and unconscious people came clearly to light. Conscious people live more in the present, see what's going on, handle difficulties efficiently and have positive personalities. Unconscious people live more in the past, do not see what's going on, find it difficult to resolve problems and have negative personalities.

CONSCIOUS SCALE

+100%   A Living Master, A Cooperative Spiritual Worker

+ 75%   An Initiate Learning/Practicing Cosmic Law

+ 50%   Knowing/Seeing, Yet Still Burdened by Personality

+ 25%   The Dawn of Awareness - Light, Beauty, Joy, etc.

UNCONSCIOUS SCALE

0%   The Struggle/The Conflict/Suffering

- 25%   The Doubters, The Sceptics, The Non-Believers

- 50%   The Mass Unconscious Who Follow The Traditions, Beliefs, Maps, Systems, Etc., of the Past without Thought.

-75%   The Assistants/Managers/Etc. Who Worship the Powerful and Fulfill Their Every Command.

-100%   The Powerful Blind Leading The Blind.

Take a look at the Conscious/Unconscious Scale above. This gives you a kind of map to work with.

Begin by holding the pendulum over the 0% point on the scale. Ask: "is (name) conscious?" If you get a yes, work your way up the scale ten points at a time until you arrive at the correct percentage range. At that point proceed one percent at a time until arriving at the exact percent of consciousness.

Knowing a person's percent of consciousness or unconsciousness will greatly assist you in handling, dealing with or relating with them in everyday life. One thing I have clearly noticed over the years, the conscious and unconscious do not mix very well, like oil and water. The conscious ones are often drained by the unconscious. It's kind of like a bird trying to fly underwater: it's impossible.

SUMMARY

1. With the pendulum there is no need for tedious, stressful, time consuming and costly testing. Our character traits emanate a vibration whether actual or potential.

2. With the pendulum you can eliminate weeks, months and even years of psychological counseling by asking a few questions.

3. Doing character analysis readings will lead to self-knowledge and insight into your character and the character of others.

4. The nature of the subconscious is to reflect and retain.

5. When a negative event is repeated over and over or has had an exceptionally powerful impact, we experience a subconscious blockage.

6. A subconscious blockage is a crystalization of life energy which interferes with the natural flow of events.

7. Follow the easy exercises for releasing subconscious blockages.

8. Psychological family patterns are made up of many energy patterns which together make up the family force-field.

9. The pendulum can be used to detect family patterns. Becoming conscious of these patterns is the first step toward breaking their hold.

10. The conscious act of detachment stops the flow of life energy into the disagreeable family pattern. Without energy the pattern will disintegrate. It will no longer affect the individual force-field.

11. Cultures and nationalities build up FORPS (Frequencies of a Race Psyche) which most people in a race psyche reflect in their personalities to one degree or another.

12. When a person's psychological nature does not mesh with his or her race psyche conflicts and frustrations take place.

13. Using the pendulum, you can easily determine the strength of identification a person has with any given race psyche.

14. A rapport refers to a negative sympathetic vibration.

15. The pendulum psychologist can track down the source of a rapport. Becoming conscious of the source usually cuts the connection between you and that source.

16. Cut the flow of negative energy before the circuit/connection is complete.

17. By consciousness I mean an acute, alert state of awareness which detects subtleties of energy, thought and feeling.

18. Conscious people live more in the present, see what's going on, handle difficulties efficiently and have positive personalities.

19. Unconscious people live more in the past, do not see what's going on, find it difficult to resolve problems and have negative personalities.

20. Checking a person's percentage of consciousness or unconsciousness with the pendulum will greatly assist you in handling, dealing with or relating with them in everyday life.

CHAPTER 13: TEACHING PENDULUM

The Learning Process

Teachers and students alike need to be aware of the learning process. Rote memorization of facts and figures is certainly not learning. Learning is more a natural unfoldment and flowering of a like or interest into thought, action and an eventual accomplishment.

The final stage in a cycle of learning is the accomplishment; and the feeling that accomplishment brings becomes the seed of a new learning process.

The teacher who believes they are successful when students accurately feedback meaningless facts and figures have missed the joys of true teaching. True teaching is a kind of magic dance with steps that have never been made before. True teaching is unpredictable, spontaneous and always responsive to the immediate thought-feeling-mood interests of the student.

True learning should be fun, exciting, exhilerating and full of energy. In that kind of an atmosphere discipline, concentration and hard work come easy.

Why does so much teaching and learning take place in a boring, stultifying, suffocating atmosphere? The primary reason is: *most teachers are not tuned-in to the learning process.*

The learning process is always and forever on the non-verbal energy level. It is what's happening. Not what happened a 1,000 years ago or what's going to happen 1,000 years from now.

Teachers who teach from the intellectual brain are like robots responding to the commands of their teachers. Everything sounds correct, at times even brilliant, but where is the feeling-energy of the moment. In an atmosphere of awareness and sensitivity facts and figures come alive.

When I was in high school I had two math teachers who exemplified the two kinds of teaching: (1) the intellectual robot (2) the aware/sensitive human.

The dry-facts-and-figures teacher gave examples, gave assignments and gave tests. It was hard to grasp dull numbers in an atmosphere of rigidity and exactness. He did not know how to make numbers come alive with interest.

The other math teacher brought exuberance and vitality to class. You felt like you were going to have a good time. He knew how to get the class laughing. We were eager to learn. He did not take teaching math too seriously.

The learning process can be broken down into 4 stages all interrelated and unfolding one from the other.

1. Interest
2. Thought
3. Action
4. Accomplishment

For instance, let's take the learning process of looking. First, is there a genuine heart-felt interest in looking? If there isn't, it's like the old adage, you can lead a horse to water but you can not make him drink.

As a cooking teacher, or a sensitive teacher of anything, do not push. If there is no interest **at this time** stop, forget it. There is a very real possibility that at some future time that person may become interested in cooking or whatever. To push where there is no interest may stifle a potential interest later on.

Once there is an interest, there must be thought. You need verbal instruction and a written recipe. The mind now has a blueprint to action.

Next, the novice cook must take action. He or she must translate thought into action. The experience of doing has to do with non-verbal sensing, muscular contractions, nerve currents, mental-emotional energies, etc.

And then, when the pie comes out of the oven you and others taste it and say it's good, accomplishment. Accomplishment then stimulates a stronger interest to become an even better cook, or anything else for that matter.

Student/Teacher Compatibility

As a parent have you ever wondered how compatible your kids are with their teachers? Sure they tell you if they like or dislike a teacher, but that is not an accurate measure of compatibility.

Do you recall Chapter 7 and the Relationship Compatibility check? (See page 64, Figure 6.) We can use the same method to find out how well a student and teacher can get along.

Once again using the 0 - 10 scale, ask: how compatible is (teacher's name) and (student's name), on the physical level?, the emotional level?, etc. After finishing the compatibility check, add up the numbers on each level and multiply by 2. That number gives you the percent of compatibility at that time.

Here's the same gradation scale that helped us categorize relationships in Chapter 7.

Superior:	=	90-100%
Excellent:	=	75-89%
Good:	=	50-74%
Poor:	=	Below 50%

If one of your kids has a poor student/teacher relationship, see what you can do to change it. In grade school this can be devastating since a child has the same teacher all year.

By the way, it should be clarified that a "poor" student/teacher compatibility does not necessarily mean a poor teacher. There's a big difference. The teacher may be excellent but when the energies come together the conditions for learning may be poor.

College students and adults taking continuing education classes can really take advantage of the student/teacher compatibility check. Usually they have more of a choice.

On an energy level what happens when a student and teacher get together? The teacher has an auric-field of emanating levels of energy. The student has an auric-field of emanating levels of energy. When the two auric-fields come together repeatedly in time, a relationship auric-field begins to form.

This third force-field becomes the teaching-field. The more conscious the teacher and student are of this teaching-field the easier and more direct is the transfer of knowledge. Enlightened teachers, masters and gurus are adept at working with the teaching-field.

Haridas Chaushin, founder and president of the California Institute of Asian Studies in San Francisco in an interview said:

> "A special transfer of energy took place during this time. A spiritually enlightened person has accumulated spiritual power and energy within him and there is an emanation, a transfer of energy between him and someone who goes to meet him in a state of receptivity. It is a power, an energy which inspires you and gives you something. In the Indian tradition, a true guru is one who can do this and does this."

A Student's Structure

What do I mean by a student's structure? In this context I am referring to a person's psychological structure. In other words, a person's way of interacting with people, places and things.

There are numerous ways of observing a person's structure. Here is one fourfold way of seeing structure:

Astrology:

Fire

Air

Water

Earth

The four primary elements of many ancient religions and philosophies, like astrology and alchemy, are an excellent functional way of seeing, sensing the different psychological natures.

Observing or thinking about the action of each element gives you an insight into that type of personality.

FIERY TYPE

They usually consume whatever it is they are involved in. They can be warm, sunny and radiant. Or they can be hot-headed, angry and fighters. Fiery types must be free to ignite and burn. Attempts to limit them can be met with rebellion. For the most part, fanning their flames (interests) keeps them happy.

AIRY TYPE

The air people breathe life into relationships. They create an atmosphere conducive to communication. They lighten things up when things get heavy. At times they are invisible but you can always feel their currents. Air cannot be bottled up otherwise they suffocate and die. Air feeds off more air. Stimulate their intellect, imagination and their understanding of peoples.

WATERY TYPE

Water always flows downhill; so, too, do watery types tend to flow into the oceans of emotion, the valleys of depression and the gutters of dispair. Water does evaporate especially when the sun shines. Watery types must be around positive people, projects and ideas in order to transmute moody water into water vapor which rises to the heavens. There seems to be no middle ground either they are flowing downhill or they are evaporating into thin air.

EARTHY TYPE

These people are the salt of the earth, the rock upon which much is built. They bring dreams into manifestation. They solidify ideas, plans/feelings and inspirations. On the negative side, earthy types can get stuck in a rut, in a routine. They can imprison themselves in a narrow lifestyle. Earthy types need to be motivated to create, to shape, to make the invisible, visible.

A teacher using the pendulum can check the element percentage of each student. In order to better guide and instruct. Begin with fiery and work your way to the earthy.

Ask: on a 0 - 100% scale what percent fiery is (name); 90 - 100%, 80 - 90%, 70 - 80%, etc. Once you determine which range of 10% then find the exact degree.

After finishing this reading you will have a fairly clear picture of that person's structure. You will know, for example, not to deal with a fiery type as if they were an earthy type - not unless you want to have a rebel on your hands.

Learning Directions

Pointing a student in the correct direction is perhaps 75% of a teacher's function. But what direction? There are so many ways a person can go.

Once you know a student's interests, background, capabilities and level of being things are narrowed down, pointing out constructive directions becomes a lot easier.

Of course, this is in a one-on-one situation; group teaching is more dynamic. Still, you can find out which direction a group would find interesting at any given time.

For many years now I have, more often than not, used the pendulum to select talk topics, books, tapes and other learning tools.

I recall one student, Ted, whose interests were so varied that it was difficult to prepare a class for him; asking the pendulum which topic he would enjoy the most that day was near impossible. By the time he got to class his interest could be completely different.

In his case, I would check the pendulum to find out three or four topics he might be interested in and then see which way he leaned when he arrived. Here's the steps I usually followed:

1. I write a student's interests and potential interests based on his/her structure; for Ted:

   ◦ Science
   ◦ Acupressure
   ◦ Math

- ◦ Reading
- ◦ Business
- ◦ Systems
- ◦ Time Management
- ◦ Etc.

2. I go down the list and ask: "Today, on a 0 - 10 scale, how strong is Ted's interest in science, math, business, etc.?

3. Those three or four topics which receive the highest reading I prepare material for.

4. When Ted arrives I look and listen to see which way the winds of interest are blowing.

5. I continually watch and listen. When the winds of interest change direction, like a weathervane, I point in a new direction.

It is amazing how much fun and complete enjoyment a teacher and student can experience when the teaching-field rhythmically breaths in this way. When a student's interest is peaked, his or her learning is usually at a peak.

The pendulum can also be used to select other learning tools like magazines, workbooks, television shows, etc. Simply write the title down or if you have the book, pamphlet, etc, hold the pendulum over it. Ask: "On a 0 - 10 scale how beneficial would X be for Ted at this time?" Work your way down from 10 until you get a yes.

The pendulum is an excellent tool for keeping a teacher alert and aware of a student's or classes' interests. Too often a teacher's plans are fixed; a textbook lays out ahead of time what is going to be covered. Unfortunately, life does not conform readily to "canned learning". The present is dynamic. What a teacher plans or a textbook presents that day may not be at all appropriate. In fact, if it is forced, it could actually retard the learning process.

Law of Co-Measurement

Most everyone I've ever talked with has had the following experience. The first day on a new job someone is suppose to show you the ropes, tell you what's going on, show you what to do. Usually, the supervisor or boss machine guns new information at you without any consideration. Your brain starts to overload. You reach a saturation point where you cannot absorb anymore.

Your boss teacher has broken a cosmic law, the Law of Co-Measurement. A consciousness can absorb just so much new information at a time. Beyond that point a teacher reverses the learning process. In fact, what has been learned can be lost because of the overload. Later the boss or supervisor wonders why you did not get the message.

A teacher must be sensitive to the student's consciousness and receptivity to learning. A sensitive teacher can feel when the student is ready for more, can feel what information and how much information the student wants and needs.

In the 19th century a very wise woman, Mary Everest Boole, wrote about what she called "Teacher's Lust". She defined "Teacher's Lust" as a blind urge to give information to students, especially information that is of strong interest to the teacher.

A teacher's strong interest is not necessarily the strong interest of the student. The teacher must be able to set aside his or her interest and pick up on the student's interest

The pendulum is a life energy measuring tool. You can tune-in in to a student's interest and find out what and how strong they are. Proceed as follows. Write down the topic being learned, say math. Then list as many areas as you can think of related to that topic.

MATH   Date:_____

- Arithmetic
- Algebra
- Geometry
- Calculus
- Etc.

As you write down the list recall what the student has said about their interest. Be sure to include that information on your list. At the end of the list write, etc. to indicate interests that you are not aware of yet. Finally, be sure to date the list. You will be re-checking it from time to time and probably adding new areas.

Now, go down the list using the 0 - 10 scale and ask: "What is (name) interest level in learning geometry at this time?" Readings of 8-9-10 indicate powerful interests.

Let's say geometry received a 9; you can proceed to find which areas of geometry may have the greatest appeal - solid geometry, analytic geometry, etc.

Now, once you have determined an area of interest you must determine how much of that topic to give at any given time. You can compare this process to hunger. Sometimes you are ravenously hungry and at other times not hungry at all.

People are hungry to learn. Sometimes they want huge does of learning, other times they are full, even though it may be a favorite topic. The teacher who applies the Law of Co-Measurement knows when, when not and how much information to give.

Students who learn from a teacher apply the Law of Co-Measurement are indeed blessed. The learning becomes joyous, energizing and regenerating. The transforming learning experience will usually stimulate a person's consciousness to pursue the limitless path of knowledge which eventually leads to understanding, wisdom and love.

Timing and Order

Timing in teaching is critical. Presenting facts and information too soon or too late can interfere with the most proficient learning level.

The conscious and sensitive teacher knows when the time is right. The teacher feels a kind of void in the students consciousness. A stream of new information floods into the teacher's consciousness and then is transmitted verbally through tones and feelings.

Most of us are not accomplished conscious teachers, that takes years of training and experience. Most of us have doubts about when is the best time to give certain information. The pendulum can pinpoint timing.

Here's how to ask. "Would it be wise for me to present X topic at this week's class?"; or this month's?, or next week's class?, etc. A yes answer - go ahead; but go ahead consciously. Be flexible. Notice changes in the student's attitudes, moods, feelings and thoughts. Adapt to the present moment.

Order in teaching is closely allied with timing. In school we depend on order from chapters in a textbook. Did you ever have the experience, like I did, of reading Chapter 8 when you were suppose to be reading Chapter 2? Chapter 8 was a lot more interesting.

It is difficult, if not impossible, to package learning into a fixed order. Obviously, in a class situation not every student can follow whatever order they want. Still, the sensitive teacher could be responsive to the class-as-a whole and set up an order more conducive to that specific group consciousness.

Also, there could be some degree of compromise to accommodate the individual's order. This could be achieved by using the pendulum.

Here's how the group and individual learning orders could be determined using the pendulum. Let's use math as our example again. The topic is arithmetic. The traditional order might be:

1. Addition

2. Subtraction

3. Multiplication

4. Division

But is the traditional order always right for every group and individual?

The key word is **always**. Life is change. Always is temporary in an everchanging world.

Write down the so called traditional order of what you are teaching. Then ask: "for this group or individual, on a scale 0 - 10 what is the wisest order?" Ten would be first, nine second, etc.

In many instances you may discover, that for now, the traditional order is the wisest. There is a natural order process which is irreversible. For instance, the seed is first; planted in soil is second. With sunshine and water, growth is third. Near the end of the growing season there's a full grown plant, fourth. The flower and fruit are fifth and sixth.

Checking the pendulum will not change the natural order.

SUMMARY

1. Learning is a natural unfoldment and flowering of an interest into thought, action and an eventual accomplishment.

2. True teaching is unpredictable, spontaneous and always responsive to the immediate thought-feeling-mood of the student.

3. True learning should be fun, exciting, exhilerating and full of energy. In that kind of an atmosphere discipline, concentration and hard work come easy.

4. When a student and teacher get together their auric-fields form a third force-field, the teaching-field.

5. The more conscious the teacher and student are of the teaching-field the easier and more direct is the transfer of knowledge.

6. A person's way of interacting with people, places and things reveals their psychological structure.

7. Observing the action of fire, air, water and earth gives an insight into the four personality types.

8. Pointing a student in the correct direction is perhaps 75% of a teacher's function.

9. Check the pendulum to find out the three, four or more topics of interest to a student at any given time.

10. A person can absorb only so much new information at a time. Beyond that point a teacher reverses the learning process.

11. Applying the Law of Co-Measurement means the precise amount of information being shared that can be comfortably absorbed and digested by a learner.

12. A sensitive teacher can feel when the student is ready for more, can feel what information the student wants and needs.

13. The pendulum is a life energy measuring tool. You can tune-in to a student's interest and find out what and how strong they are.

14. Students who learn from a teacher applying the Law of Co- Measurement are indeed blessed. The learning becomes joyous, energizing and regenerating.

15. The conscious and sensitive teacher knows when the time is right. The teacher feels a kind of void in the student's consciousness. A stream of new information floods into the teacher's consciousness and then is transmitted verbally through tones and feelings.

16. Order in teaching is closely allied with timing. The sensitive teacher sets up an order most conducive to learning.

CHAPTER 14: SPIRITUAL PENDULUM

Tuning to the Spiritual Frequencies

There are many rewards coming to those who work with the pendulum: concentration, emotional calm, direct experience of the frequency world and an incredible awareness of human psychological dynamics.

Beyond all this, the greatest reward I have enjoyed is the joy of tuning to the spiritual frequencies. How? You do not have to ask any questions. Write down what or who you want to tune-in to. Hold the pendulum. Hold the thought.

If your concentration is steady and your emotions are neutral you will begin to feel the spiritual frequencies. It may take repeated practice to consciously feel the frequency you're tuning to. The spiritual frequencies are super-subtle.

At first you may not know what spiritual frequency you want to tune-in to. May I suggest the "Univeral Divine Presence". This spiritual frequency is omnipresent throughout the cosmos. The Presence is ubiquitious. It flows through this book, your body and the room you are now in.

A 17th Century French lay brother, Brother Lawrence, from the Order of the Carmelites practiced for more than forty years tuning to "The Presence". Brother Lawrence's conversations and letters were published in a little booklet, **The Practice of the Presence of God** in 1701. If you ever come across a reprint,by all means buy it. It is a treasure.

Brother Lawrence summed up his experience by saying, "in Thy Presence is fullness of joy."

For many years now I have had the privilege of tuning to the Eternal Presence. My friends, I am not talking about blind faith or emotional religious feelings. I am talking direct experience. You do not have to have someone experience **The Source** for you.

At this moment I recall a difficult time in my life. I was breaking up with the woman I loved; I was nearly broke; I was working in a job I hated.

Still, I had a membership at a local health club. Almost every night, after a hard day's work in Midtown Manhattan, I stopped for a swim, a sauna and tuning to the Eternal Presence.

There was a kind of relaxation room with a half dozen massage tables. The lights were low. No one talked. I tuned my mind to the Presence. I held it there. I began to feel the burdens of the day leave, my breathing became fuller and more rhythmic. The tensions left. I began to feel a part of everything.

By the time I got dressed and walked home I was a new man. I didn't have a care in the world. I could look at my problems and solve them more easily.

I can't say it any better , "in Thy Presence is fullness of joy."

The Energy Centers

Interpenetrating the physical body is a dynamic energy body. The function of the energy body is to circulate prana or life energy through the physical. Without the rejuvenating life energy, the physical body deteriorates. When life energy stops circulating through the physical body life on this level ceases.

There are seven major energy centers strategically placed in the energy body. Each center vibrates and radiates another life sustaining energy. The seven centers are located in relations to the physical body as follows. See figure 12 on page 135.

Crown Center	Spiritual Energy
Brow Center	Conscious Energy
Throat Center	Communication Energy
Heart Center	Giving Energy
Solar Center	Emotional Energy
Spleen Center	Desire Energy
Sacral Center	Regenerative Energy

The seven major centers are named variously in different religions, philosophies and initiation orders. For more important than the name is the function. Different energies are focused and funneled through each center. It is quite easy to see where a person is identified, in terms of centers, by the way they act.

Now, it is common for an energy center or centers to become blocked, clogged or polluted with negative energy. When we go against our structure, our natural flow of energies, we detune our energy centers.

As a pendulumist you can determine which centers are balanced and which unbalanced. Use figure 12 on page 135. Hold the pendulum over each

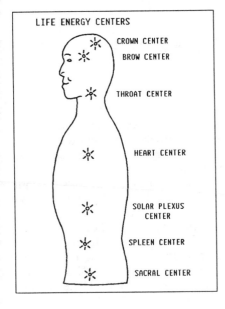

Figure 12: Life Energy Centers.

center and ask: "on a 0 - 10 scale, how balanced is John Doe's crown center at this time? Descend from 10 until you get a yes answer.

One or more centers may be unbalanced at a time. Unbalanced centers radiate inharmonious energies. The strong tendency is to attract, like iron filings to a magnet, exactly what you are emanating. The result: a vicious circle of unbalanced energies in a center.

In the long run the imbalances may cause mental and emotional fixations or possibly even physical disease.

How do you tune the centers? There are numerous ways. One method I was fortunate to come across recently is fairly easy and remarkably effective.

It is part of the regenesis healing technique developed by Bob Rasmusson. Begin with the brow center. Take the first two fingers and thumb of your right hand and place them on the point between your eyebrows. Next, hold your left palm down, just above the crown center.

The next step is the key. Breath in through the nose to the count of one and out the mouth to the count of six.

Proceed to each center and repeat the process. If your left arm gets a little tired drop it for a moments rest and return into position. Stay with each center for as long as you feel comfortable, one minute to several minutes.

Once you work on each center there is one last step. With the hands 4 - 6 inches from the front of your body alternatingly pass your hands up the torso from the spleen center to the throat center. Make 50 or so passes.

How do you feel after the energy center balance? If it works for you, use it.

Meditation

There are three stages in the process of beginning meditation:

1. Preparation
2. Practice
3. Conclusion

In meditation you must reverse the usual flow of attention energy. Instead of directing your attention through the senses onto the outer world you want to quiet or neutralize the senses so that your energies flow into your inner world. This brings us to the preparation stage.

Choose a quiet place where there is plenty of fresh air. Make sure your clothes are comfortable, not too tight fitting so that the circulation is free and easy.

Sit comfortably in an upright position. In other words, keep your body erect. Do not slouch. Spine and neck should be in a straight line.

Next, you want to relax the body. Let go of the excess tensions wherever you might sense them: back of the neck, jaw, shoulders, legs, etc. As an Egyptian master of meditation said, "the real process of meditation begins when the student has attained the ability to still the body."

Now, close your mouth. Breath ever so gently through the nostrils, inhaling and exhaling rhythmically. Once you begin the breathing, close your eyes and observe the breathing cycles. Do not try to control them.

With a relaxed mental attitude begin a gentle, natural withdrawal from perceptions of the world and thoughts of day to day problems.

You have reached stage two of meditation: practice.

Choose a meditation object (m.o.) from nature. For example, seashells, plants, stones, pinecones, eggs, etc. You can choose your m.o. before the meditation process or when the practice stage begins. If you like, just before meditation, look at the m.o. so that your mind has a fresh image.

The pendulum can be used to help select a m.o with which you have a strong vibrational affinity.

Now, make a clear, detailed m.o. image on the screen of your mind. The m.o. gives the mind something upon which to focus attention, so that the mind does not wander excessively. Allow the mind to revolve the meditation object in every direction, developing its possibilities.

At this point, do not strive for results. Avoid impatience. Pay no attention to any disturbing sounds.

Remain aware, observing, detached, poised and centered. Allow free movement. Refuse to be carried away by any wave of thought or emotion. But, if you are suddenly carried into a fantasy, immediately let go of it and resume the position of a detached onlooker.

The secret of meditation success lies in keeping the mind steadily on its plane and subject, but leaving it free within the limits of that subject. An operation that takes considerable experience and skill.

Beginners often notice the continuous rise and fall of thoughts. If you are determined in your training they will eventually disappear. If you find yourself giving in to the tendency to fall asleep, daydream or become blank, you have gotten off the track. Simply snap yourself back to attention.

Keep stage 2, meditation practice, to approximately 5 - 10 minutes a day. If possible, choose the same time each day. Use your pendulum to determine how long is wise for you from day to day.

Now, you have reached stage three, conclusion.

Open your eyes slowly. Bring your full attention back to your normal everyday activities. If any flashes of inspiration or intuition have come to you, write them down. All your findings in meditation must be checked and tested before accepting them as facts. In the meantime, you may assume the attitude of insufficient data.

Generally, it is not wise to indiscriminately communicate your inner experiences because there's the danger of inflating your ego by exaggerating the facts. Also, it can dissipate the energy of meaning.

One final suggestion offered by a sage: "It is in ordinary life that we develop our qualities and our meditation as a science is best kept very close to that."

Levels of Being

There are many levels of consciousness. Using the pendulum you can discover which level a consciousness is most identified. The predominate consciousness level is a person's level of being.

The levels of being can be divided several ways. In this instance I will break them down into seven levels from the most conscious to least conscious.

Level of Being:

1. Formless Divine Presence - 10%
2. Synthesis of Consciousness - 5%
3. Light Beings - 30%
4. Higher Mind - 50%
5. Energy World - 20%
6. The Psychic Levels - 10%
7. Blind Thought, Desire, Action - 5%

Hold the pendulum over each level. Ask: "What percentage of consciousness is focused on level 1, level 2, level 3, etc.; 90 - 100%, 80 - 90%, etc."

Write down the percentage on each level as above. Do you notice any tendencies? Where are most people focused? Were you able to do your reading without prejudice?

If you are not that familiar with each level you might want to read the next couple paragraphs before you attempt to check the predominate level of being.

The Formless Divine Presence was described in the first section of this chapter, Tuning to the Spiritual Frequencies. "In Thy Presence is fullness of joy".

Synthesis of Conscious is the being of beings. All awareness combined into one consciousness, the father-mother god consciousness.

Light Beings refers to individualized beings who function in light bodies and circulate the light throughout the dimensions.

Higher Mind is the focal point of patterns, seeds and forms which manifest in the energy and matter worlds.

The Psychic Levels are the planes of reflected patterns, seeds and forms. The Higher Mind could be compared to an alpine peak and surrounding landscape. And the Psychic Levels would be the reflection in a still mountain lake.

Total identification with Blind Thought, Desire and Action is equivalent to unconsciousness. The inner being is imprisoned in false images, material things and the physical body.

This was a capsulated definition of each level. Become conscious of each level. By holding your attention on any given level you tend to experience the vibrations on that level. First hand experience, when possible, is almost always better than someone elses verbal description.

As you become more conscious of each level you will be able to receive more accurate readings on the Level of Being. You will begin to notice what level you are focused on most of the time. And, you will be more conscious of what level those around you are on.

Knowledge, Wisdom, Love, Understanding

Exploring the spiritual frequencies with the pendulum can be the adventure of a lifetime. So far most of the questions have been aimed at knowledge; a properly worded question can result in answers that enlighten.

As you use the pendulum more and more it dawns on you: tune-in and you receive an answer. I purposely used **an** answer instead of **the** answer. Knowledge is not written in stone.

Under different circumstance, a different frame of mind, a different state of consciousness, the answer changes, sometimes only slightly, sometimes a great deal. That's one reason, throughout the book, I have emphasized the *"when index"*; date your questions and answers. Things change.

Beyond questions and answers, beyond knowledge and information, the pendulum can assist you in tuning-in to spiritual vibrations. Love, wisdom and understanding can be experienced directly. You simply must have a steady attention, emotional calm, physical repose and sensitivity to vibrations and energy.

Do these skills sound familiar? If nothing else the pendulum can help you to develop the spiritual faculties.

Now, to tune-in to love vibrations hold your pendulum over the word love. Hold you attention. Go into neutral like when you ask a question. Now, though, instead of asking a question you hold your attention on love.

Feeling the love frequency should be instantaneous. Remember how you felt the energy when you asked questions? You are still a receiver. Be sensitive to the love energy.

For some people it can be quite a revelation to discover they can feel love without being in love. The love frequency permeates the universe. To hold a fixed thought that love occurs only when romance blooms is restrictive. You have access to love whenever you choose to feel it.

Wisdom is another spiritual frequency. Wisdom is the conscious and measured application of knowledge to specific life situations. Wisdom is a frequency-field that can be felt, experienced and applied.

Again the process is the same. Hold the pendulum over the word wisdom. Hold your attention and tune-in. What do you feel? Do your perceptions change?

You may not sense the wisdom vibration immediately; it depends on how sensitive you are. Continue; practice tuning-in to wisdom. Gradually you will pick up the wisdom energy.

In the Old Testament of the Judeo-Christian Bible it is written, "and with all thy getting, get understanding." No doubt about it, understanding is a mighty force. Understanding erases the hatred between nations, peoples, families and individuals.

Understanding is the conscious feeling of another's feelings, thoughts and experience and then the complete acceptance of other's feelings, thoughts and experience.

Understanding demands more than simply holding your attention, and tuning-in. You must make an effort to put yourself in the other person's place. You must, for a moment, think and feel the way they do. At that moment of awareness understanding can occur.

The Christ/Buddha Frequencies

In Buddhist literature I came across the following wise statements:

1. "What you worship you become".

2. "Don't worship the Buddha, Become a Buddha."

When you idolize, praise and think a lot about a certain hero you tend to become much like that person. You begin to dress alike, think alike, act alike. This is most evident in the case of Elvis Presley impersonators. Teenagers have their rock musicians and sports heros.

When you worship someone or something too much you relinquish your own individuality. You no longer follow **your** process of unfoldment and enlightenment. Someone elses way replaces your way. As a result **you** stop growing.

Statement two, "don't worship the Buddha, become a Buddha" is a corollary to statement one. The wise Buddhist knows the danger in excessive imitation. Naturally, at a certain evolutionary level, when a person is identified with the psychic nature, they tend to reflect and imitate others.

The Buddhist knows that eventually an individualizing Buddhist must find his own way - stop worshiping the Buddha and become a Buddha.

With the New Age emerging it is time to stop worshipping the Christ personality, Jesus, and begin evolving and then awakening the Christ Consciousness within ourselves.

The days of so called spiritual intermediaries holding the power over millions of followers is coming to an end. It is time for each to follow his or her path. No two paths are the same. Although our paths cross and often cross again, we must each be perceptive and intuitive enough to find and stay on our path.

You do not have to wait any longer for a Christian priest or a Buddhist monk to tell you what the Christ or Buddha Consciousness is like. You can tune-in to the Christ/Buddha frequencies yourself directly - NOW!

The pendulum can be used as a consciousness raising tool. Write down Christ or Buddha Consciousness. Follow the same steps you have throughout the book.

1. Come to attention, a state of wordless awareness.

2. Become emotionally neutral, neither for nor against.

3. Hold your attention steady.

4. Be sensitive and receptive to the Christ/Buddha frequencies.

SUMMARY

1. There are many rewards coming to those who work with the pendulum: concentration, emotional calm, direct experience of the frequency world and an incredible awareness of human psychological dynamics.

2. May I suggest tuning-in to the "Universal Divine Presence". This spiritual frequency is omnipresent throughout the cosmos.

3. Interpenetrating the physical body is a dynamic energy body or subtle body. The function of the energy body is to circulate prana or life energy through the physical body.

4. There are seven major energy centers strategically placed in the subtle body. Each center vibrates and radiates another life sustaining energy.

5. When you go against your structure, your natural flow of energies, you detune your energy centers.

6. Unbalanced centers radiate inharmonious energies. The tendency is to attract exactly what you are emanating. The result: a vicious circle of unbalanced energies in a center.

7. One way to tune the centers is to use the regenesis healing technique for balancing the centers developed by Bob Rasmusson.

8. There are three steps in the process of meditation: 1. Preparation 2. Practice 3. Conclusion.

9. In meditation you must reverse the usual flow of attention, energy. Instead of directing your attention through the senses onto the outer world you want to quiet or neutralize the senses so that your energies flow into your inner world.

10. The secret of meditation success lies in keeping the mind steadily on its plane and subject, but leaving it free within the limits of that subject, an operation that takes considerable experience and skill.

11. Using the pendulum you can discover on which level a consciousness is most identified. The predominate consciousness level is a person's level of being.

12. Review the seven levels of being from most conscious to least conscious.

13. As you become more conscious of the levels of being you will notice which level you and others are focused on.

14. Beyond questions and answers, beyond knowledge and information, the pendulum can assist you in tuning-in to spiritual vibrations.

15. Love, wisdom and understanding can be experienced directly. You simply must have a steady attention, emotional calm, physical repose and sensitivity to vibrations and energy.

16. When you worship someone or something too much you relinquish your own individuality. You no longer follow **your** process of unfoldment and enlightenment. Someone elses way replaces **your** way. As a result you stop growing.

17. With the New Age emerging it is time to stop worshipping and awaken the Christ Consciousness within yourself.

18. You do not have to wait for a Christian priest or a Buddhist monk to tell you what the Christ or Buddha consciousness is like. You can tune-in to the Christ/Buddha frequencies yourself directly - NOW!

CHAPTER 15: NEW AGE PENDULUM

New Agers Incarnating

Many born since the late seventies are New Agers. The old age vibrations are absent. These New Agers do not have to go through a long transition from an old age orientation to a New Age view. They are born tuned-in to the New Age.

What do I mean by New Agers? A New Ager, or Aquarian soul as they are called by astrologers, functions according to energy, vibration, frequency and perception. Old agers tend to function according to symbols, signs, images, words and dogmas.

The New Agers incarnating, literally by the millions, will not put up with the false images, false hopes and false ideologies being pushed and sold by old age hucksters greedy-for-wealth and the power that goes along with it. Within twenty years New Agers will begin to outnumber old agers in many parts of the world. The New Age young ones will refuse to identify with the tricks of the greedy and powerful, then the greedy and powerful will have few to be greedy and powerful over.

The young ones, who may be older in terms of being, are naturally drawn to New Age learning. Astrology, energies, auras, spiritual frequencies, light beings are natural inclinations.

Just a few weeks ago I was visiting a friend. She has a gifted three year old daughter, Amber. We were asking some business questions. Her daughter was fascinated with the pendulum but, I thought, no more so than any other three year old.

About a week later Amber came into the office with her mom. She went almost immediately to a pendulum which, by the way, was not exactly in plain sight. I sensed her natural interest and gave her a pendulum.

About another week went by and my friend began to tell me how fond Amber was of her pendulum. She treated it very special. When she was done playing with it she always put it away, which was not a common practice with the rest of her toys.

Parents should become aware that many children are naturally attracted to the pendulum, astrology, auras, new age music and the like. If possible, encourage their interest. You do them and yourself a favor. If you don't encourage them they will come to it anyway. You may as well go with the flow.

The New Agers incarnating need special attention and care. Their spiritual interests demand recognition. They require regular doses of New Age spiritual frequencies. Without these rejuvenating energies, watch out. They will drive you crazy until you listen and give them what their heart desires.

Nothing is Hidden

If every person, place and thing radiates energy and you can tune-in, register and feel the energy then -- nothing is hidden! This is an awesome statement. Nothing could be kept from you. Whatever is top secret can be known instantly. No one could hide from you. Lies could be detected easily. Deception would be obvious.

The pendulum is one New Age tool that can shed light on the so called hidden. The pendulum sees through, behind and beyond the image, the surface and the superficial. Your consciousness will see beyond the veils. Your awareness will know no boundary.

Old agers are secretive. Their "hidden" knowledge becomes a power over others. Imagine for a moment - a doctor, lawyer, scientists, etc. spends years of schooling to learn what you can tune-in to and experience directly in seconds. When more and more people discover the frequency universe these old age authorities will lose their power.

That's not to say that all doctors, lawyers and scientists will disappear in the New Age. Far from it. Rather, there is a radical change of consciousness going on even among the Old Age powerful.

Many are discovering the frequency world too. By knowing more directly and quickly using a pendulum they can benefit others more readily and more cost effectively.

Have you ever been awestruck by being in the presence of a rich, famous or powerful person. We tend to project false images and false ideals onto these people. When you can tune-in to what is - to their vibrations - you know them without talking with them or meeting them. In fact, you can know without ever seeing them in person.

In the comfort of your own home you can tune-in to world, national and local leaders and find out their present psychological condition. You can determine the percentage of accuracy of any newspaper, television or magazine report. You can check the authenticity of any so called fact.

When nothing is hidden from you, you realize you cannot hide anything from someone else who sees. Then you feel a connection to All That Is. You begin to experience humanitarian vibrations. You know and then understand your fellow human beings more than you ever have.

You begin to realize; why hide what cannot be hidden? Your "darkest secrets" are easily seen by seers of energy. In fact, to them they are that more obvious because they are secrets. They stick out like sore thumbs.

As we stop hiding from ourselves and then from each other, the old age games of deception, illusion, delusion and confusion are not played much anymore. With that, love and understanding root themselves in the soul. They grow and blossom into sharing, caring and giving. The light shines in the darkness. Our path up the mountain of enlightenment shines bright.

Tele-Pendulum

Doing readings over the telephone has become a common practice for me. Friends, clients and close associates have experienced accurate results with tele-penduluming.

One time a student called with an urgent question. His car broke down and he needed to select the most qualified yet inexpensive car mechanic. He gave me three names. I used the 0 - 10 scale reading. I received a nine on one mechanic. He used him and found fast, fair priced service.

Recently a woman friend was searching for a job. I told her to call me every Monday morning and read me the job descriptions from the classifieds which seemed interesting to her. I would jot down a few key words and ask: on a 0 - 10 scale how compatible is Betty with this job? She claims this helped her narrow the field down each week.

Tele-penduluming is not much different than the usual pendulum questioning. The person asking the question is across town, across the country or on the other side of the world. That is the only difference.

Sometimes pendulumists who first do tele-penduluming have a fixed concept which blocks them from being open to long distance vibrations. It may seem a little strange to be tuning-in to energies thousands of miles away.

Think about this for a moment. Does it seem strange that your television set picks up satellite signals thousands of miles away and a picture appears? Most of us take it for granted.

I have said repeatedly throughout the book every person, place and thing emanates energy. If you can tune-in to the wavelength of that person, place or thing you can feel-experience it regardless of distance.

I have known pendulumists who are called to answer health questions and to check patient doctor compatibility. One thing to be aware of here - people with urgent health questions are usually emotional. If you started picking up emotional energies, be sure to begin slow rhythmic breathing through the nose in order to detune some from their interference. Emotionalism will almost always throw off your answer. Sometimes it might be wise to get the question and tell them you will call them back with the answer in a few minutes.

New Age pendulumists will not have to travel great distances to feel the energies in a special place or know where a particular person is at. In fact, it is not necessary to even be in contact over the phone. Hold your attention, practice emotional calm and be sensitive to what you pick up.

New Age Groups

As your path to the lighted heights winds its way through earthly time you attract New Age groups. How do you decide whether or not a group's influence will be constructive or destructive?

New Agers have a distinct love of freedom. They do not want some group dictating their every step along the way. On the other hand New Agers do want to learn from others and share what they have learned with others.

Over the years my path has crossed many groups some constructive, many destructive. I have used the pendulum to assist me in discriminating which is which.

I recall several instances where a group had an excellent image and reputation but the pendulum indicated it was not wise for me to participate. Members of a group, whose leader had written several well received books, asked me to come speak at their national retreat. It seemed like a great opportunity.

I didn't consider asking the pendulum. I went ahead and planned a trip. The day I was supposed to leave a major snowstorm dumped two feet of snow. The trip was off.

I scheduled the trip a few months later. When the day came to leave the car broke down. Strike two!

It was about time to pull out the pendulum. I asked, "on a 0 - 10 scale how wise is it for me to speak at the xyz retreat?" The answer -- a surprising 1. No wonder the resistance was so great.

Well, I recently traveled to the area of the country where this group had its retreat. I decided to check it out first hand.

After asking directions from someone in the nearby town, I headed for the retreat. I must have missed a turn because I ended up driving miles down a dirt road.

I finally turned back. Intuitively, I spotted the location tucked in a grove of trees. Their sign was little help since it was small and only had the group's initials.

When I reached the main building and grounds I understood why the pendulum only registered a one. The vibrations were a turnoff. The place was broken down. The people were unkept and unfriendly. I stayed only a few minutes.

Now, if you're looking for a local group to share and learn with, make a list of as many as you can find. Using the 0 - 10 scale ask, "How compatible am I with x, y, z group?" Once you get an 8, 9 or 10 ask, "would it be wise for me to participate every week, once a month, every once in awhile?"

Be sure to update your readings on a regular basis. Things change.

A positive group can have an uplifting influence. The support, shared experience and loving understanding provides stability. A negative group can undermine your individuality, take away your freedom and seduce you into a mob consciousness.

Humanitarian Pursuits

New Agers not only want to evolve individually they want to serve others. New Agers want to contribute to the evolution of the planet-as-a-whole.

A New Age pendulumist can find out where their energies can best be utilized in humanitarian pursuits. Simply ask the question and see what the pendulum says.

As the New Age energy field manifests more and more completely in the coming years. The beliefs, ideals and institutions of the old age will pass away completely or be totally transformed. We already see evidence of this trend in religion, politics, economics, education, etc.

How can you and I contribute consciously to the revolutionary change process?

First, each individual must see the trends clearly. The pendulum will assist you in seeing. Make a list of the major life areas:

Religion	Military
Politics	Health
Economics	Arts
Education	Literature
Science	Etc.

Go down the list. Ask a series of questions in each area. The answers will enlighten you. Your awareness will expand, ultimately giving you a subtle sense registering coming changes.

Let's check the science area as an example. How does the rate of scientific discovery in the 20th century compare to the rate in the 19th century on a 0 - 100% scale? In other words a 100% answer would mean double the rate and so on. I got a 900% increase. What percent of the world's scientists are mostly controlled by greedy, power hungry business people and/or politicians? 65 - 70%. Obviously the list of questions could go on for pages. Remember, the idea is to become more aware of what's going on.

Next, you must find an area where you can contribute. Using the same list ask the following question. On a 0 - 10 scale how effective would I be in devoting my energies to X area? Answers of 9 or 10 mean get involved in that area.

Finally, you must set a course of action, you must do something to contribute to the process of change. Use the pendulum to assist in setting your course and steering you around obstacles.

Pendulum Life Reading

Over the years friends, associates and students have asked for counseling sessions using the pendulum. What gradually evolved was what I now call the "Pendulum Life Reading".

The Pendulum Life Reading is a series of charts which are spiral bound into a 8 1/2 x 11 booklet. The charts include:
- ° Wheel of Whole Living
- ° Circle of Subconscious Blockages
- ° Relationship Compatibility
- ° Health Maintenance Dial
- ° Character Analysis Chart
- ° Pendulum Color Spectrum
- ° Astro-Energy Scope
- ° Life Energy Centers
- ° Questions (all the questions you want to ask)

I reserve space for comments on each page. I offer specific suggestions for overcoming conflicts, frustrations and problems.

The beauty of the Pendulum Life Reading is the tuning-in to the immediate energies in the present. I use a 0 - 10 scale. On most charts I word the question as follow: "on a 0 - 10 scale how balanced is (Name) at this time?

When I get an answer of 5 or below I give practical ways of balancing the energy. This way the client is not left hanging, wondering what they can do. The advice offered can also be checked to see how wise it will be.

The Pendulum Life Reading does not predict the future. It focuses primarily on the present energies and memories of the past that may be blocking the flow of present energies.

I am very careful to date each reading. I explain to the client that I'm picking up energies a certain way today. I tell them that if they change their attitude, desire, feeling, thought etc. then the reading would be different.

I have done hundreds of Pendulum Life Readings. Most have expressed positive thoughts about the accuracy and immediate benefits.

It does not take months and years to pinpoint psychological difficulties. With the pendulum they can de discovered in a matter of minutes.

I usually do the actual questioning before the client arrives for the appointment. All I really need is their name.

It is difficult for some to comprehend how I can receive answers when they are not present. I often reply by asking them how do they see television pictures broadcast invisibly through the air?

"I turn on the TV and I see them," they often answer.

I then say, "the human mind - nervous system is a sensitive receiver of vibrations and energies. Just as a television is a structured receiver of images and sounds. Everything, everyone, every place in the cosmos emits energies. The mind knows no boundaries. By focusing attention on something, on someone, the mind is in immediate sympathetic vibration."

The Pendulum Life Reading is one way New Agers can gain self-knowledge. By becoming conscious of present conditions the chances of moving forward constructively is increased a thousand-fold. One of the greatest difficulties in life is the tendency to get stuck, to locked into a difficult problem.

Once solidly identified with the frustration we become blind to present conditions. The Pendulum Life Reading tends to disburse the cloud of gloom and doom.

In the New Age now upon us we need ways to clarify with some immediacy. Talking about a problem for endless hours is the habit of the old age. In the New Age we want to know and we want to know now. And not only do we want to know now, we want to know what to do about it now!

SUMMARY

1. A New Ager functions according to energy, vibration, frequency and perception.
2. New Agers will not put up with false images, false hopes and false ideologies pushed and sold by old age hucksters greedy for wealth and the power that goes with it.
3. The New Agers incarnating need special attention and care. Their spiritual interests demand recognition. They require regular doses of New Age spiritual frequencies.
4. The pendulum sees through, behind and beyond the image, the surface and the superficial.
5. When more and more people discover the frequency universe old age authorities will lose power.
6. When nothing is hidden from you, you cannot hide anything from someone else who sees. Then you feel a connection to All That Is.

7. Tele-penduluming is not much different than the usual pendulum questioning. The person asking the question is across town, across the country or on the other side of the world. That's the only difference.

8. If you can tune-in to the wavelength of a person, place or thing you can feel-experience it regardless of distance.

9. If you're looking for a local group to share and learn with, make a list of as many as you can find. Using the 0 - 10 scale ask, "how compatible am I with x,y,z group?

10. A positive group's support. shared experience and loving understanding provides stability.

11. New Agers want to contribute to the evolution of the planet-as-a-whole.

12. Using a pendulum you can find out where your energies can best be utilized in humanitarian pursuits.

13. First, become aware of world conditions. Next, find an area where you can contribute and finally, set a course of action.

14. The beauty of the Pendulum Life Reading is the tuning-in to the immediate energies in the present.

15. The Pendulum Life Reading is one way New Agers can gain self-knowledge. By becoming conscious of present conditions the chances of moving forward constructively is increased a thousand-fold

For further information on Pendulum Life Readings write:

Life Energy Sciences
316 California Ave., Suite 210
Reno, Nevada 89509

APPENDIX 1

PROPER BREATHING

Rhythmic Breathing
The Full Breath
Stop Smoking
Improve Air Circulation
Negative Ion Generator
The Mountains

Seashore
Pine Forest
Desert
Exercise
Fresh Air
Etc.

RESTFUL SLEEP

Fresh Air
Stop Automatic Thinking
Bed Direction (North/South,
    East/West)
Relaxation
Kind of Bed
Room Energy Environment
People Sleeping Nearby

Herb Tea
Sunshine
Eeman Circuit
Massage
Meditation
Prayer
Warm Milk
Etc.

TOXIC HYGIENE

Water
Food
Chemicals
Toothpaste
Deodorent
Soaps
Color Television
Computer Terminal
Power Lines

Transformers
Underground Streams
Faults
Lead
Carbon Monoxide
Drugs
Nicotine
Etc.

SUFFICIENT EXERCISE

Swimming
Walking
Bicycling
Tennis
Golf
Skiing
Baseball
Basketball
Volleyball

Rowing
Canoeing
Aerobics
Jogging
Running
Football
Hiking
Soccer
Etc.

RELAXATION

Meditation
Eeman Circuit
Rhythmic Breathing
Therapeutic Massage
Shiatsu
Acupressure
Swedish Massage
Chiropractic Adjustment
Zone Therapy
Music
Color
Drawing
Painting
Gems
Hydrotherapy
Reflexology
Relaxation Exercises

Camping
Picnicing
Traveling
Vacationing
Flower Remedies
Crystals
Positive Energy Plates
Multiwave Oscillator
Stretching Exercises
Hatha Yoga
Loving Relationships
Relaxed Sitting
Relaxed Standing
Biofeedback
Smiling
Laughing
Etc.

NUTRITIONAL DIET

Fruits
Vegetables
Vitamins
Minerals
Fresh Water
Mineral Water
Herbal Tea
Juices
Milk
Cheese
Nuts/Seeds
Beans
Proper Cooking

Food Combinations
Nutritional Balance
Digestion
Elimination
Colonics
Fish
Chicken
Beef
Pork
Turkey
Grains
Etc.

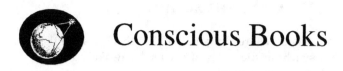 # Conscious Books

- Books & Tapes by Greg Nielsen

- Pendulum Life Readings

- Astrology charts

For information on ordering write:

Conscious Books

316 California Avenue, Suite 210
Reno, Nevada 89509

ABOUT THE AUTHOR

Greg Nielsen has been "treading the path" in this life since the 60's. Through a synchronistic series of events, he awakened to psychic and spiritual experiences.

Visions, dreams, vivid perceptions, chakra awakening, masters teachers and the school of hard knocks have organically shaped his spiritual spiral.

Greg is the co-author of two international best-sellers, **Pyramid Power** and **Pendulum Power.** His book **Tuning to the Spiritual Frequencies** emphasizes the skills required in order to continually tune to the spiritual while in the midst of every day life. He wrote **MetaBusiness: Creating a New Global Culture** to assist others in the process of applying spiritual principles to business, career and work.

Greg also practices and teaches astrology. He does a daily radio feature, **Greg Nielsen, Your Guide to the Stars.**

Greg Nielsen is available for talks, workshops, seminars, speaking engagements and book signings for your group, bookstore or organization. For information on ordering a Pendulum Life Reading, Astrology Chart, books and tapes write:

Greg Nielsen
c/o Conscious Books
316 California Ave., Suite 210
Reno, Nevada 89509